ENTREPRENEURS INSIDE

Sarah,
To a true
corporate entrepreneur.
Susan Foley

ENTREPRENEURS INSIDE

*Accelerating Business Growth with
Corporate Entrepreneurs*

Susan Foley

Library of Congress Control Number: 2007901924
ISBN: Hardcover   978-1-4257-5161-6
                   Softcover   978-1-4257-5157-9

This book was printed in the United States of America.

To order additional copies of this book, contact:
Xlibris Corporation
1-888-795-4274
www.Xlibris.com
Orders@Xlibris.com
38547

In memory of my parents, Harriet and Tom
who inspired me with their love and encouraged me
to follow my dreams—they were the best.

Table of Contents

Expanded Table of Contents

Acknowledgment

Thanks to all the corporate entrepreneurs who contributed to this book and encouraged me to write it. They inspired me with their stories, their courage and their insights. This extraordinary group of individuals has stepped up to the challenge of moving their companies forward into the future. They openly discussed their triumphs and defeats, and talked about their personal and professional aspirations. They expressed their concerns and doubts, and shared their hopes and desires for their organizations. They wondered if anyone really understood what they were all about, and were eager for their organizations to know.

This book has taken me on an exciting journey that started when some former colleagues encouraged me to follow my passion, test my hypothesis, and search for the truth. I am grateful to them for lighting the spark that encouraged me to pursue the topic of corporate entrepreneuring more closely. My former bosses gave me the opportunity, freedom and funding to build new and innovative solutions for our customers. They inspired and encouraged me to think that anything was possible. The colleagues who challenged what we were doing only made us more determined to succeed. My employees weren't always sure where we were headed but were eager to come along for the ride.

Thank you to my business associates—I am grateful for your insights, wisdom and contribution to this effort. I also thank my friends, who supported and encouraged me as I've moved forward. I also thank my brother, who believed there was one more new venture to pursue; Tom, who has been there for me every day and long night; my mother, who supported everything I did; and my father, who taught me how to be a pioneer. I am grateful to all of you.

My education and work experience laid the foundation for this book. I was fortunate that early in my career I worked for two of the most entrepreneurial companies at the time, 3M and Hewlett-Packard. They both left an entrepreneurial imprint on me that stayed with me throughout my career. It wasn't until a few years ago that I even understood what the phrase "corporate entrepreneur" meant. Then it dawned on me one day that what I was—and had been my entire career—was a corporate entrepreneur.

I would like to extend my deepest thanks to all the people who have been a part of this effort in some way, at some point. Beth Allan of Phoenix Marketing International; Jamie Arking of Quest Diagnostics; Mike Balin of StreamServe; Judy Banker of Gatti & Associates; Suzanne Bates of Bates Communication; Linda Bentley of Business Visions Inc.; Jim Bluhm of Moen Incorporated; Charis Borchers of The Devine Group; Teri L. Cavanagh of TLC Connections; Joe Chiavarini of Business Technologies; Jonathan Cleveland of Cleveland Associates; Celia Couture of CC Consulting; David Dickinson of CEO4Rent; Doug Dickson of New Directions; Vicki Dolan of Boston Women's Business; Michael F. Donnelly of Donnelly & Associates; Cynthia Ferrone Eletto of The Pilates Studio; Amanda N. Ellis of International Finance Corporation; Leo J. Esposito; Brian Foley of PMA Insurance Group; John Friar of Northeastern University; Sheri Woods Green of Minds-I International; Shelley E. Hall of Catalytic Management; Sarah Hammann; Mary Hildebrandt of Razors Edge; John Kerr of Kerr Editorial; Rik Kranenburg of McGraw Hill Publications; Kevin Lefler of The Devine Group; Jeanne Lewis; Ken Lizotte of Emerson Consulting; Suzanne Lowe of Expertise Marketing; Sue Pace McKay of Battalia Winston; Rick McPartlin of Design Sales In; Brendan McSheffrey of Fuel Dog; Linc Miller of Sandler Sales Institute; Rex Miller; Carol Mofford of Initial Stage Consulting; Andy Paul; Marie Pouliot of Andover Management Group; Tom Price of Focused Project Management Inc.; Anna M. Ratajski of Quest Diagnostics; Sydney Rice of The Boston Coaching Company; Marc-Andre Roy of R3D Information & Technology; John L. Rueter of StreamServe; Caryn Saitz of Creative Strategic Solutions; Rosalyn Acosta Sayre of Sovereign Bank; Sandra Seagal of Human Dynamics; Willow Shire of Orchard Consulting; Brehn L. Smith of Business Transfers & Strategies LLC; Katherine Tallman; Ann P. Tangen of State Street Corporation; Martin Tannenbaum; J. Chrisann Taras of A.J. Edwards; Sandy Thomas of Innovative Strategies Group; Tammy Torrey of Torrey Designs; Kathleen M. Victory of Blue Pencil Consulting; and Bill Wagner of Accord Management Systems.

Thank you.

Introduction

Atop priority for many CEOs is business growth through innovation. Yet beyond the hype, the results from innovation are disappointing. Many CEOs do not think that they have the skills and capabilities to accomplish their growth agenda. They want to transform their organizations to become more entrepreneurial but it is proving elusive. Despite this, the Bureau of Economic Analysis estimates that spending on innovation and new products would reach $2.1 trillion dollars in 2006/2007.

Much of the focus today is on entrepreneurship and its manifestations, those external organizations or start-ups created by entrepreneurs who have an innovative idea they want to exploit. Entrepreneurship inside organizations is called corporate entrepreneurship or Intrapreneurship, and refers to the formal and informal process of investing in new business initiatives, products or services, or business processes inside an existing organization. It is estimated that more than fifty percent of new ventures are created inside existing organizations.

Both entrepreneurship and corporate entrepreneurship are a viable means of creating business growth and stimulating the economy. They are similar in many respects and different in others. This book focuses on corporate entrepreneurship and the most effective way to build corporate entrepreneurship as a core competency. Corporate entrepreneurship provides the framework to support innovation and business growth.

Much of the academic research and business literature has been focused on entrepreneurial start-ups. As a result there is limited research in the area of corporate entrepreneurship, although this is changing thanks to a handful of progressive universities doing research in this area. The available research is a useful starting point for understanding corporate entrepreneurship, but it does not go far enough in defining the obstacles and hidden barriers to successfully implementing corporate entrepreneurship in an existing organization.

A key part of the problem is that many corporate executives still don't fully understand the difference between corporate entrepreneurs (Intrapreneurs) and entrepreneurs. The available research in the area of corporate entrepreneurship suggests that each group uses different processes, each representing a unique set of challenges and opportunities. Combine this with the shortage of role models at the top who fully understand the dynamics behind corporate entrepreneurship and you can see why organizations have not tapped into this valuable resource.

Entrepreneurial talent alone is not enough, but it is a starting point. In her article "The Age of Entrepreneurial Tolerance," Elizabeth W. McBeth at the Joseph L. Rotman School of Management, University of Toronto, put it this way: "The most sought after professional for the 21st century economy will be a breed of corporate entrepreneurs, or Intrapreneurs, whose education and experience are both broad and deep and who have the skills for identifying and exploiting opportunities, fostering team-based innovation, creativity, and managing change."

Many companies may be letting significant growth opportunities slip by because they are not effectively harnessing the most able business builders they've got: their corporate entrepreneurs (Intrapreneurs.) The lack of focus in many companies on this very important role and the limited research are key impediments to leveraging this valuable resource. The long-term consequence: a talent drain that is steadily robbing companies of whatever entrepreneurial edge they may have had.

There is no need to dwell on why entrepreneurial skills are needed in Corporate America today. Read any Wall Street analyst's report and you'll hear the growth drumbeat right away. Nor is it necessary to repeat the calls to institutionalize corporate entrepreneurship as a way to gain a competitive advantage.

Aligning an organization's systems and processes to support corporate entrepreneurship is critical to building entrepreneurial capabilities. Existing systems and processes often thwart an organization's efforts to become more entrepreneurial. Resistance to change is one key obstacle; others include funding, a lack of commitment, and short-term focus. Developing corporate entrepreneurship as a core competency takes time and practice to perfect. The best way to become entrepreneurial is to *be* entrepreneurial. Experimentation and action learning are the two ways to accelerate your organization's learning.

As an experienced corporate entrepreneur, I was frustrated by the lack of reference material that actually looked inside the world of the corporate entrepreneurs. Most of the material was written by individual observers about the process, instead of by the participants who actually experienced the process. Reading about the theory provides a solid foundation, but it does not provide the essence of what it is like to see the process through the eyes of corporate entrepreneurs. It does not matter what you call them—corporate entrepreneurs, Intrapreneurs, mavericks, positive deviants, business builders or entrepreneurial leaders—this book was written for them with help from them.

A group of experienced corporate entrepreneurs across a diverse set of industries participated in this book's development. They were senior executives, many who reported directly to the CEO. Some were responsible for building billion dollar businesses in their organizations. Some managed their own business units and were committed to building the entrepreneurial capabilities within their own group. A few managed multi-million dollar technology investments, some managed incubators and others created their own skunkworks in the core business.

They contributed their time to the development of some of the corporate entrepreneuring tools discussed throughout the book. They shared their experiences of being corporate entrepreneurs, their greatest achievements and biggest disappointments. They provided new insight and understanding about what it means to be a corporate entrepreneur. They found comfort in knowing others who understood what they were going through. They were intelligent, highly motivated and energized about being a corporate entrepreneur, and they encouraged the writing of this book. I am grateful for their time, wisdom, and enthusiasm.

My goal is to provide you with the best insight, real-world experience, and truths that make corporate entrepreneurship one of the most exciting and motivational things your organization can do to achieve new business growth. Unlike some of the textbooks that lay out the theory behind corporate entrepreneurship, this book will take you inside the world of corporate entrepreneurship. You will see corporate entrepreneurship through the lens of the entrepreneurial leader, the team, and the organization.

My intent is to offer an insider's view of the challenges and opportunities that corporate entrepreneurs will face, and the roles and responsibilities of entrepreneurial leaders in ensuring that the corporate venture thrives inside the organization.

Chapters 1, 2 and 3 provide an overview of corporate entrepreneuring. Theses chapters explore corporate entrepreneuring as a business process, the entrepreneurial framework needed to support it, navigating organizational obstacles and the use of project management to instill discipline. Chapters 4, 5 and 6 take a look at the behaviors, competencies and dynamics of the key players; corporate entrepreneurs, entrepreneurial leaders and teams. Chapters 7, 8 and 9 look at the three key building blocks of corporate entrepreneurship; creativity, innovation and change. Chapter 10 looks at the ultimate end game, execution.

If you are an executive trying to integrate the entrepreneurial spirit into your organization, this book will help you understand how to do it. The book will discuss ways in which you can evaluate your organization to see how entrepreneurial it is. It can help you identify key individuals in your organization who have the potential to be entrepreneurial leaders.

If you are a professional who is unsure whether you are a corporate entrepreneur, you will gain better insight into the attributes of a corporate entrepreneur. You will be able to relate to real-life examples of how corporate entrepreneurial teams operate and how they deal with uncertainty, adversity, and resistance.

If you are working in an academic institution, I hope that this book will inspire you to continue to do more multi-disciplinary research on corporate entrepreneurship.

Every day that goes by without utilizing your company's entrepreneurs is a day further away from reaching your growth goals. Let's get started with a look at corporate entrepreneurship.

Chapter 1

Explore the Next Frontier

Corporate Entrepreneuring

1.1   Catalyst for Growth—corporate entrepreneurship is the *catalyst* for business growth

1.2   Elusive Butterfly—there is a lack of a clear *definition*

1.3   Growth Process—complex *business process* that crosses organizational boundaries

1.4   Foundation for Success—*people, process and place* to support business growth

1.5   Pioneers—the *individuals* that make things happen

1.6   Extraordinary Leaders—a unique combination of *competencies*

1.7   Building Blocks—underlying fundamentals of *creativity, innovation and change*

1.8   Hitting the Target—the ability to execute with *precision*

Corporate Entrepreneur Insights and Lessons Learned

1.1 Catalyst for Growth—*Corporate Entrepreneuring*

Corporate entrepreneurship is a business process that transcends all aspects of the core business and serves as the catalyst for business growth. The goal of corporate entrepreneurship is to build organizational capabilities and competencies in order to accelerate business growth. Organizations with strong entrepreneurial orientations statistically perform better than traditional organizations. Institutionalizing entrepreneurship can be an effective way to gain a competitive advantage, and being more entrepreneurial will help you attract and retain highly talented knowledge workers. Experimenting with entrepreneurship will help increase your success rate. *Corporate entrepreneurship is the catalyst for business growth.*

Corporate entrepreneurs or Intrapreneurs are the engines of growth. They provide the energy, drive and motivation to help your organization grow. They possess a unique combination of competencies, enabling them to work effectively in an entrepreneurial environment. They have the required depth and breadth of experience to deal with the complexity and ambiguity that is an integral part of entrepreneurial initiatives. They are relentless in their desire to learn and grow. Corporate entrepreneurship provides them with the type of environment in which they thrive.

Innovation is seen as the springboard to business growth. Despite the hype about it, the failure rate of innovation remains high. Innovation alone is not enough. Corporate entrepreneurship provides the necessary infrastructure for successful innovation. Higher levels of innovation yield greater market share, new product revenue, improved profitability, technical dominance, improved process and cost control, and greater shareholder returns.

The term "corporate entrepreneurship" is an oxymoron. Unlike an entrepreneurial start-up that is created as a stand-alone entity, corporate entrepreneurship is created inside an existing organization. It challenges traditional organizational practices and forces the organization to hold a mirror up to itself to see what it has become. You will find that embedding corporate entrepreneurship into an existing organization requires a major transformation. It is all about change.

Corporate entrepreneurship requires managing the inherent tension between maximizing economic value and developing human capital. Resources and control systems will have to be realigned to support corporate entrepreneurship. You will need to develop new practices for evaluating opportunities and managing risk. Customer intelligence will be more tightly integrated into your decision-making process. There will be a shift in traditional and rational approaches to hiring. You will need to find new ways to maintain the entrepreneurial behavior needed for competitive success.

Although business growth is the overall end game, you will find that corporate entrepreneurship is difficult to achieve. Corporate entrepreneurship is not included in most of the theories, models or frameworks that have been developed to guide managerial practice. There is a limited understanding of the relationship of entrepreneurship to change, creativity, and innovation—the building blocks of corporate entrepreneurship.

Leaders typically find themselves in uncharted waters and lack the guidelines on how to direct or redirect resources toward entrepreneurial strategies. Traditional management practices don't apply. Entrepreneurial leadership requires a shift in thinking and behavior. There is often a lack of entrepreneurial role models at the senior management level to provide direction. It is not a lack of talent but a lack of experience with these types of entrepreneurial endeavors that is missing.

Entrepreneurship can be extremely threatening to the people that do the work. Most of the research on individual characteristics and behaviors has been done on start-ups and independent entrepreneurs. There is currently no consensus in the academic and business world about what makes a good corporate entrepreneur. Corporate entrepreneurs and entrepreneurial leaders are hidden talents in many organizations. This book describes new research on the behaviors and competencies of corporate entrepreneurs.

Corporate entrepreneurship will vary depending on the type of initiative, new business, product or service, or process. You will be developing the process as you move forward. There are a number of different obstacles and hidden barriers you will encounter along the way. You will have to find ways to work with and around existing systems and processes. No two initiatives will be the same.

The research conducted to date has identified some of the more pervasive constraints on corporate entrepreneurship. They include everything from an absence of innovation goals, lack of commitment from senior executives, no entrepreneurial role models, and misdirected reward and evaluation systems to long and complex approval cycles, lack of consensus on priorities, and a resistance to change. These issues provide a starting point for understanding some of the obstacles and barriers you will encounter along the way.

Many corporations are not prepared to institutionalize corporate entrepreneurship. There are no benchmarks, metrics or performance criteria for corporate entrepreneurship. Many executives do not know why new initiatives succeed or fail. A failure rate of fifty percent for new initiatives is deemed acceptable. The reasons behind success or failure are often unique to each institution. Understanding the fundamentals around project and program management can go a long way in helping to set up the infrastructure and discipline for tracking and measuring progress.

If you want to create an environment to accelerate business growth, corporate entrepreneurship is one way to accomplish that. It takes a commitment of time, resources, and experimentation. You must be willing to live with ambiguity and tolerate failure as part of the learning process. There is no silver bullet for becoming entrepreneurial overnight; it takes practice and having the right people, processes and infrastructure to support and sustain it over time.

Corporate entrepreneurship can be the catalyst for business growth, but only if there is a commitment to it. Those organizations that have been successful in building entrepreneurial capabilities have reaped the rewards and perform better.

Is your organization committed to becoming more entrepreneurial?

1.2 Elusive Butterfly—*Definition*

It makes logical sense to start with a definition of "corporate entrepreneurship," but the problem is that there is currently no consensus on one. So it is not surprising that the term itself is so misunderstood and confused with the better-known term "entrepreneurship." You may remember that when business process reengineering became the hot topic, some people saw it as a fundamental restructuring of business processes, while many others viewed it as cost cutting in disguise. *There is a lack of a clear definition.*

A simple definition for corporate entrepreneurship is:

> The formal and informal process of investing in new business initiatives,
> products and services or business processes inside an existing organization to
> drive business growth.

Breaking this definition apart, the key words are:

- formal (sanctioned by the corporation) or informal (skunkwork)

- process of investing (venture-funded, budgeted or hoping to get funding)

- new business initiatives (building a brand-new business)

- products and services (creating a new revenue stream)

- new business processes (strategic redesign or realignment of business processes)

- inside (corporate venture group, division or separate entity)

- an existing (established) organization

- to drive business growth (revenues, profits, market share).

Given the lack of a clear definition, let's use the above throughout this book. You are probably saying, "Okay, this definition makes sense, but it sounds a lot like business as usual." It is and it isn't. The real difference is determining whether you are creating something brand-new or making enhancements or extensions to an existing business, product, service or process. If you are entering new territory, then it would be considered corporate entrepreneuring. If you are making enhancements to something that already exists, then it would be considered an improvement.

Within the context of corporate entrepreneurship are the concepts of radical innovation and incremental innovation. Radical innovation often refers to the development of new businesses, products, or services that set new standards of performance and have the potential to dramatically impact price, performance, or cost. Incremental innovations are often seen as improvements to existing businesses, products, or services that provide smaller improvements in price, performance, or cost. Radical innovations have higher risks and higher rewards.

New business initiatives often fall outside of the traditional budgeting process. Many companies set up an internal venture group to fund new, high-risk, longer-term investments. Some firms set aside budgets for new initiatives. Some firms have separate R&D groups or incubators solely focused on developing new business opportunities for the company. Seems straightforward but it isn't. There is a lot more complexity when breaking new ground, whether it is a new product, technology, market or customer segment. All of these opportunities create new challenges and higher risk than the organization may be prepared to deal with.

Corporate entrepreneurship is the foundation required to support the development of these brand-new initiatives. Unlike other business processes that might follow a standard work process, corporate entrepreneurship will vary by organization. Corporate entrepreneurship is often seen as a chaotic process that takes shape as it moves along. In reality, it is a change process or transformation that pushes the existing boundaries and tests the limits of organizational systems and processes.

Although there are numerous areas where you can apply corporate entrepreneurship, the three main areas you will want to become familiar with are new businesses, new product and service development, and new business processes.

A new business initiative refers to the creation of a business that is new to the world or new to the company. The company is venturing into uncharted waters. Typically they will have limited or no experience in the market or with the customers they are targeting for the new business. It often requires a bigger leap of faith and more due diligence on the company's part. Tolerance and adequate funding are also key variables when breaking new ground.

New product development refers to the creation of a new product line or service that did not previously exist in the company. These are products and services that were conceived, designed, and developed to address an unmet need in the market. Of course all companies have ongoing product development efforts, but many of them are focused on enhancements to or new versions of existing product and service lines.

The area of new business processes is a little trickier. Many businesses have done an excellent job of redesigning their business processes to streamline their operations and cut costs. Many of these improvements have been to existing processes. You can think of new business processes as a strategic shift in business direction. It is a time when an organization repositions or realigns itself to take advantage of new market opportunities that were not previously available given their earlier operating style.

Keep in mind that these are simple definitions and should suffice until there is a more definitive definition of corporate entrepreneurship. They do, however, serve as a baseline for understanding some of the challenges of corporate entrepreneurship.

Until there is a clear consensus on a definition of corporate entrepreneurship, you might want to create your own definition.

A key component of creating an entrepreneurial environment is developing a definition that makes sense to your organization and your strategic goals.

What is your definition of corporate entrepreneurship?

_____

1.3 Growth Process—*Business Process*

Corporate entrepreneurship is not a separate function like marketing or finance; it is a business process designed to accomplish a specific task over a period of time to achieve a stated goal. Corporate entrepreneurship is a complex process that touches all aspects of the organization including strategy, organizational structure, policies and procedures, systems, culture, people and customers. Think of it as overlaying a new process across all of these dimensions. *It is a complex process that crosses organizational boundaries.*

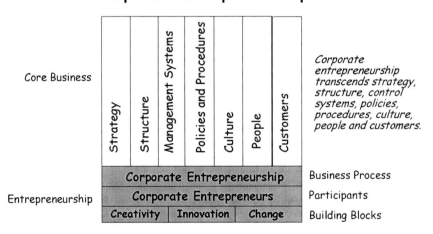

Each dimension is well established and deeply entrenched to support the core business. As you build your entrepreneurial capabilities, you will find that these dimensions are in conflict with your entrepreneurial goals. You will have to change some of them, and simply tweak others.

The actual process is similar to creating an entrepreneurial start-up, but it requires creating the new initiative within the context of the existing organization. Like a start-up, the new initiative will deal with a shortage of resources, time pressures, and financial constraints. If you decide to set it up as a separate entity within the organization, then you will need to establish new guidelines. You'll also need to identify sponsors who can provide on-going support. The CEO and executive team will have to be involved in promoting it and giving it political capital.

Unlike other business processes, the steps for corporate entrepreneurship will vary depending on whether you are building a new business, creating a new product or service, or strategically redesigning your business processes. Each step will be heavily influenced by the characteristics that define your existing organization.

As a result, there is no right way or perfect way to implement these business processes. There are, however, three underlying principles that provide the foundation for corporate entrepreneurship: developing individuals with entrepreneurial skills and capabilities, developing the operating framework or processes to support corporate entrepreneurship, and creating an entrepreneurial mindset and infrastructure.

Do you have a process in place for corporate entrepreneurship?

1.4 Foundation for Success—*People, Process and Place*

People—*Entrepreneurial Competencies*

Creating an entrepreneurial mindset and having an operating framework in place are important, but they only provide the structure and process—not the motivation, commitment and drive. The human system elements of corporate entrepreneurship are the critical success factors that often make the difference between success and failure. "Human systems" refers to the "soft stuff": the people, the culture, and the processes that support the individual and collective needs of the team.

The heart and soul of corporate entrepreneurship are the individuals that drive these initiatives. It is their belief in making a difference, their commitment to the project, their ability to work effectively in teams, their trust in the leader, their skill at dealing with complexity and their confidence in doing what's needed to get things done.

These are the things that make all the difference. Yet they are often the very things that are given the least amount of attention.

Implicit in all of this is having individuals with the right skills to drive these new initiatives. A major issue is the shortage of entrepreneurial role models at the top to drive these initiatives. There is also a limited ability to identify and develop corporate entrepreneurs, due in part to the lack of a clear definition of what makes a good corporate entrepreneur. These individuals have a unique combination of skills and competencies with different motivations and aspirations than most employees.

Corporate entrepreneurs are individuals that thrive in an environment of change. They have a thirst for knowledge and aggressively seek out opportunities that enable them to grow. They get bored easily and enjoy creating things that are new and exciting. They have little tolerance for the status quo and prefer to work in a challenging environment.

You are most likely to find them working on the front end of a new business, product, or service initiative. They enjoy the thrill of seeing something move from concept through development. They often lose interest when it comes to taking that business or opportunity to the next stage of business growth or beyond to managing a mature business. So it is not surprising that there may be an exodus of these individuals out of organizations.

If you look at all the academic research and business journals, you will find a list of skills and attributes. If you talk to corporate entrepreneurs, you will find a more robust and realistic assessment of their skills, capabilities and attributes. The following list is a consolidation of the competencies that are deemed most important for corporate entrepreneurs, based on research and interviews with experienced corporate entrepreneurs.

Core Competencies

Corporate Entrepreneur Profile™	
· Accountability	· Motivating
· Adaptability	· Navigating Uncertainty
· Challenge/Growth/Change	· Passionate Communication
· Collaborative	· Problem Solving
· Engaged and Thriving	· Strategic & Analytical Thinking
· Execution	· Takes Action
· Independent Thinking	· Team Builder
· Leadership Effectiveness	· Tolerance for Stress
· Market/Customer Focused	

On the surface, you may think these seem like the same competencies of leaders—and you are right. Many of these competencies are critical success factors for CEOs and executive leaders. There are, however, a few but important differences between the competencies of corporate entrepreneurs and CEOs. The difference is found in the underlying behaviors that combined make up these competencies and the degree to which they are needed to perform the job.

The Devine Group is a behavioral assessment firm that has spent 35 years looking at the behaviors of successful people. They currently have a database of over 100,000 success profiles. The Corporate Entrepreneur Profile™ was developed in collaboration with The Devine Group to focus specifically on the behaviors and competencies of corporate entrepreneurs. The tool was designed by and developed for experienced corporate entrepreneurs.

The Corporate Entrepreneur Profile™ is not based on personality traits or cognitive thinking styles, but on behaviors. Personality is something that you develop over time and is not easily changed. You can think of it as what you "can do." Behaviors, on the other hand, are a reflection of what you "will do" and are more easily changed.

You may want to consider using a combination of assessment tools to better understand the behaviors, personalities, thinking styles and motivations of individuals with entrepreneurial tendencies. You will find that developing entrepreneurial skills and capabilities requires taking an introspective look at oneself.

The more you understand about human dynamics, the better prepared you will be to deal with unexpected issues, conflicts, and confrontations in the group, in the organization, and with key stakeholders.

What are you doing to develop entrepreneurial competencies?

Process—*Operating Framework*

Organizational systems and processes often thwart attempts to become more entrepreneurial. Existing systems and processes get in the way and performance metrics penalize growth efforts. Business program management practices are weak or non-existent and there is limited ability to execute successfully. Learnings are not captured so lessons learned are not passed on. You must identify and modify all of these obstacles to create an operating framework that supports corporate entrepreneurship.

As the process of corporate entrepreneurship has evolved, so has the understanding of some of the reasons for its success and failure. The following diagram illustrates a number of challenges that you will face as you begin to implement corporate entrepreneurship in your organization.

Major Challenges

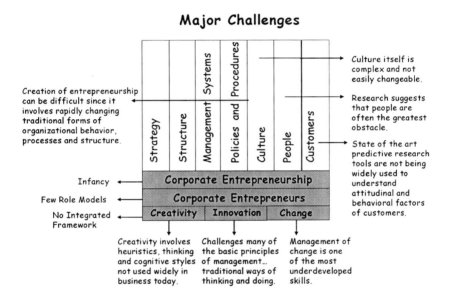

The following are some of the higher-level organizational issues that you will encounter as you embark on corporate entrepreneurship.

•   Corporate Entrepreneurship—is still in its infancy

•   Intrapreneurs—there are few role models

•   Creativity—involves heuristics, thinking and cognitive styles

•   Innovation—challenges many of the traditional ways of thinking and doing

•   Change—is one of the most underdeveloped skills

The biggest barriers to corporate entrepreneurship are a short-term focus, lack of time and resources, bench strength and culture. These are major hurdles to overcome, so it is not surprising that the failure rate of new business initiatives is so high.

A fundamental premise going in is that corporate entrepreneurship will require adherence to existing organizational processes. Many of these existing processes will either support the initiative or impede its progress. Evaluating these processes in terms of a framework that supports corporate entrepreneurship will highlight critical factors and issues that you must address before moving forward.

First, you need to understand the potential issues and hidden barriers that are likely to get in the way. Second, you need to look at performance metrics that can be used to support an entrepreneurial venture. Third, you need to establish outcome measures that can be used to track and measure success.

The Corporate Entrepreneuring Audit™ provides a baseline for evaluating your existing systems against the needs of the new venture. The framework looks at business processes across organizational boundaries and functions to determine if they are in alignment. It forces you to take a hard look at the existing organizational practices and adjust them to fit the needs of the new initiative. It will enable you to look at the effectiveness and maturity of each process in terms of supporting the overall goals of the new initiative.

The audit will help you define and create your own operating framework.

Operating Framework

Corporate Entrepreneuring Audit™	Strategy	Structure	Systems	Policies Procedures	Culture	People	Customers
Barriers to Success							
Performance Metrics							
Outcomes							

You will find that some existing policies and procedures may be too constraining, organizational structures might get in the way, or management systems may be too rigid. Measurement systems may be unrealistic, the culture may not be conducive to innovation, employees may see this as a career-limiting opportunity, and your customers may not welcome the change.

There is no one answer to why so many new business initiatives fail. There are a million reasons why they could fail. It is a complex web of interrelated activities that combined cause the failure. Understanding why they fail is as important as knowing why they succeeded. Failure and experimentation go hand in hand. Failure seeds success.

All of these issues will surface eventually, so dealing with them before they occur will save you a lot of time and money down the road. The end goal is for you to create an operating framework that the meets the needs of your new initiatives.

What type of operating framework will work for your organization?

Place—*Entrepreneurial Mindset and Infrastructure*

Creating an entrepreneurial mindset and infrastructure is by far the most difficult challenge. Corporate entrepreneurship does not naturally occur in organizations. It requires an environment that most leaders are not accustomed to dealing with. It requires changing the very people who are so heavily invested in the core business. Organizations find it far easier to continue feeding the cash cow than to rock the boat. It also forces the organization take a hard look at what it has become and that is often very unsettling.

Corporate entrepreneurship requires discipline to be effective. Many corporate entrepreneurial initiatives are project-based, so adhering to proven project management practices can be very useful. If you work for an organization that has a project management orientation, you will want to leverage those aspects that make sense and drop those that will get in the way. You will need to find the right balance of discipline while leaving room for creativity.

Business program management is often a much greater need in organizations than project management. Business program management refers to the management practices that must be in place to support large investment initiatives. Business program management is targeted at executives and provides a framework for strategic oversight of large investments. It is used when investments are high-risk or will have a significant impact on a company's financials. You are probably doing some form of business program management if you use portfolio management, risk management, change management, benefits management or similar management tools.

Both project management and business program management are important. The key is instilling organizational discipline in support of corporate entrepreneurship. There are several things that senior management can do and many things the team can do to improve their effectiveness. Experience is the best teacher and action learning is the best way to develop entrepreneurial competencies. Working on real business problems or new business opportunities provides the focus and motivation for participants.

Commitment from the CEO and senior management is an imperative. Without their support and involvement throughout the process, it is doomed to fail. It takes political capital that only the CEO can provide. If you don't have business sponsors willing to be actively involved as coaches and advisors you will find it tough going. If they are not strong enough to stand up to the powers that be, then they will not be able to see you through the tough times.

Trying to establish corporate entrepreneurship without a roadmap is a recipe for failure. It will be important for you to have the right tools and techniques to support your efforts. You will need a roadmap that structures the learning process. You will want to leverage processes and practices used by successful companies. Implementing a proven process will get everyone on the same page. Developing and using a common language will be important for streamlining communication and getting everyone to understand the implications of their decisions.

The Corporate Entrepreneurial Infrastructure™ was developed to address these needs. It is an executive workshop designed to build the entrepreneurial mindset and infrastructure you will need to support corporate entrepreneurship as a core competency. It provides a roadmap with the tools, techniques and processes to solve business problems or evaluate new business opportunities. It has been used successfully in some of the world's largest organizations to develop the behaviors and discipline required to embed corporate entrepreneurship into your culture.

Entrepreneurial Mindset and Infrastructure

Corporate Entrepreneurial Infrastructure™			
Create Entrepreneurial Mindset	Define Operating Framework	Develop the Roadmap	Final Presentation
Opportunities/ Problems	Alternatives	Validation	Solution

The goal is to establish corporate entrepreneurship as a core competency, transform the way your organization works, and more effectively grow the business. It will help you develop new leadership skills so that you can operate differently, develop cross-functional capabilities and accelerate business growth. It will help you develop empowered, accountable teams with skin in the game who can develop quick, fact-based solutions. You will build an environment of openness to new approaches and breakthrough thinking. These capabilities will provide quality assurance and deliver solutions that solve strategic business problems or create new growth businesses for the organization.

Corporate entrepreneurship is a process that evolves over time. It is a competency that must be learned, shaped and customized to the unique needs of your organization. It requires a commitment of time and effort on the part of the CEO to push through walls and break down barriers. It requires adequate funding, a long-term view, and a portfolio approach to managing investments over various time horizons for corporate entrepreneurship to succeed.

If you want to build an entrepreneurial mindset and infrastructure, you have to make it a strategic priority. Experimentation is the best way to build the skills and capabilities you will need to develop corporate entrepreneurship as a core competency.

Does your organization have an entrepreneurial mindset and infrastructure?

1.5 Pioneers—*Corporate Entrepreneurs or Intrapreneurs*

Corporate entrepreneurs are the classic in-house counterparts of classic entrepreneurs. They build new revenue-generating products and services and sometimes whole new business entities within existing organizations. They are calculated risk takers, avid learners, and deal effectively in an environment of change. Corporate entrepreneurs regularly blaze trails through uncharted territory. *They are your organization's pioneers.*

As a rule, corporate entrepreneurs are skilled individuals who are interested in working for something greater than themselves; making a difference usually matters more to them than climbing the corporate ladder. As a corporate entrepreneur you will have to deal with policies, procedures, management systems and measurements that may not always support your efforts. You will have to cope with resistance, isolation and lack of peer support. You will bump up against the entrenched bureaucracy and may have to break rules to get things done.

Corporate entrepreneurs are independent thinkers who are looking for meaning at work. They see corporate entrepreneurship as a way to test their skills, flex their muscle and push the edge of the envelope. Corporate entrepreneurs strongly believe in what they are doing and are focused on the end goal. They are creative and find innovative ways to solve problems. They are the creators, doers, and implementers who make things happen.

Corporate entrepreneurs are dedicated to the project and loyal to the team. They recognize the value of diversity, commitment, and trust. They work effectively as individual contributors and team members. They may not like everyone, but they respect people for their contributions. They collectively create a new entrepreneurial culture inside the existing organization.

During the late 1990s, many organizations lost their entrepreneurial talent to start-ups. Others, under pressure to control expenses, have redirected entrepreneurial resources to business-as-usual efforts. So finding a corporate entrepreneur isn't easy. Potential employees who think they can do the job often underestimate its complexity. It is important to recognize that a corporate entrepreneur must possess organizational skills and values that are not required for an independent entrepreneur. So how exactly do corporate entrepreneurs walk and talk?

Corporate entrepreneurs are creative. They are motivated and energized when creating and building something new. They are the early adopters of ideas. They see ideas not for what they are but what they can become. Corporate entrepreneurs are individual contributors interested in creating value and moving the company forward. As a result they gravitate toward those projects at the beginning of the business development lifecycle.

If you look at the typical lifecycle of a business, most corporate entrepreneurs prefer working in the start-up phase. The real thrill for them is getting the business, product or service going. They take pride in seeing it get launched. They often have little or no interest in taking it to the next level of growth. They much prefer to work on the next new project.

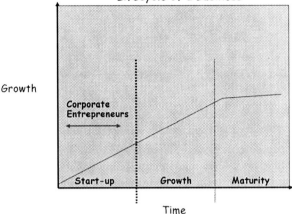

This is a simple way of identifying corporate entrepreneurs, but it helps in understanding why certain behaviors and competencies work best in this type of environment. It will also help you understand why some corporate entrepreneurs decide to leave once a project is completed.

Some of the behaviors and competencies you should look for in corporate entrepreneurs are:

- Ability to deal with unexpected challenges

- Thrives in an environment of change

- Takes initiative to follow through and honor commitments

- High tolerance for stress

- Displays willingness to take risks

- Holds self and others accountable

- Establishes effective working relationships

- Strong self-awareness

You can also do a quick inventory of individuals by using the list of seventeen core competencies for entrepreneurs listed in Appendix A.

The Corporate Entrepreneur Profile™ is a more comprehensive view of the 33 behaviors and 17 competencies. The profile looks at behaviors that are critical, important, and nice to have. The 33 behaviors are then grouped and weighted according to their importance for a particular competency.

The goal is to build a team that has a mix of all the 17 competencies. This way you will have the right balance of behaviors to enable the team to be the most effective. In the end, it is the team's strength and determination that is the deciding factor between success and failure. We'll include more discussion about the behaviors and competencies of corporate entrepreneurs in Chapter 4.

What processes are in place to recognize and develop corporate entrepreneurs?

1.6 Extraordinary Leaders—*Entrepreneurial Leader*

Entrepreneurial leaders have a breadth and depth of experience that often transcends that of those who followed traditional career paths. They understand their companies' overall goals; they know where the corporate boundaries are unyielding and where they can flex. They are passionate about creating new opportunities that fit the business strategy, and they can ably marshal and energize resources to create those opportunities. *These individuals have a unique combination of competencies.*

These individuals are not always the inventors of new products, services or processes, but they are very often the team builders who turn those ideas into profitable businesses. They are seen as the business architects who design the work environment, create informal controls, provide the discipline, and drive the change by promoting entrepreneurial behavior in others. They open channels of communication, and establish clear roles and responsibilities, goals and measures.

Entrepreneurial leaders are change agents; they have a high tolerance for ambiguity, prefer autonomy, have plenty of perseverance, and are committed to making a difference. They are goal-oriented, self-motivated and decisive. They are willing to push the limits of what is acceptable behavior to get things done. Their motivation and behaviors mean that they inevitably run up against entrenched bureaucracies. They face plenty of resistance, isolation, lack of encouragement, and issues of control. They are often forced to challenge policies and procedures.

Their leadership style lends itself to networking, building relationships, and empowering employees to achieve results. They encourage diversity, promote collaboration, and strive to empower individual team members. They are also emphatic and attuned to the individual and collective needs of team members. They are often independent thinkers and have strong opinions and belief in what they are doing. They are committed to the task and dedicated to completing the mission.

In light of the above traits, there are many who say that anyone can be a corporate entrepreneur but there is little evidence to prove that one way or the other. There is, however, evidence that certain behaviors and competencies can determine success. These are often better indicators of who is best suited for the role of corporate entrepreneur. Traditional leaders thrive in environments that support the core business, but corporate entrepreneurs relish the opportunity to create something new. They languish, however, when it comes to maintaining or sustaining a business.

The real difference between traditional leaders and corporate entrepreneurs may be in the experience itself. A corporate entrepreneur will encounter new hurdles along the way, including hitting the wall, traversing the valley of despair, or flying blind. These experiences will bring profound changes to the individuals involved. It will change who they are and who they have become. They will have a hard time stepping back into old roles or behaviors.

Entrepreneurial leaders make the transition to a new way of working that is foreign to the rest of the organization. Asking them to go back to the core business will be unsettling. Asking them to help institutionalize what they've learned will inspire them.

Not only are these leaders' good entrepreneurs, they are also good employees. They are committed to serving the company and the new initiative. They must live in two worlds at the same time: the entrepreneurial venture and the core business. It is as if they have one foot in one boat and one in another. They must find the right balance when organizational pressures, resource constraints and funding issues of the existing business come in conflict with the new initiative.

These are just a few of the traits that entrepreneurial leaders must possess. We will discuss other traits and how you can identify them in your leaders in Chapter 5.

Who are the entrepreneurial role models in your organization?

1.7 Building Blocks—*Creativity, Innovation, and Change*

The building blocks of corporate entrepreneurship are creativity, innovation and change. These building blocks are rooted in separate academic disciplines, which add to the complexity of understanding their role in corporate entrepreneurship. Each of these building blocks has its own process. They overlap in some places and they are separate in others. Academic researchers are now beginning to take a multidisciplinary approach and studying the relationships and interactions between these building blocks.

Creativity is rooted in the discipline of psychology and refers to idea generation. The ideas themselves can be developed in various ways through the R&D process, brainstorming, or intuition. Creativity is a starting point and an ongoing process of refinement and fine-tuning. Individuals with creative minds are often right-brained thinkers. They leverage their intuition and they see patterns and synergies between independent variables. They see the gestalt.

Innovation is the integration of new ideas into products, services, processes and practices and refers to the introduction of a new idea, method or device that has commercial value. The term "innovation" in business is most often thought of in terms of a new technology or a new use for an existing technology. Radical innovation refers to creating something that never existed before and would come from R&D. More incremental innovations emerge from practice.

Change is rooted in the discipline of organizational development and refers to doing things differently. The process of change can relate to people, process, relationships, culture, etc. It often requires that both the entrepreneurial team and the core business change their thinking, behavior, and mode of operating. Resistance to change is one of the biggest obstacles. Change also refers to supporting new ways of working and eliminating ways that get in the way.

The following illustration explains the interrelationship between the building blocks and their relationship to corporate entrepreneurship, product/service development, and product/service management.

Building Blocks of Corporate Entrepreneurship

Corporate entrepreneuring provides the context for support of these building blocks. Many organizations are jumping into innovation without having the fundamentals in place to support it.

- Corporate entrepreneuring refers to the organizational process of creating new businesses in established companies.

- Creativity refers to the process of creating new ideas and thoughts that become the fuel for innovation.

- Innovation refers to taking those ideas and integrating them into new business, product, or service concepts.

- Change refers to the ability, willingness, and need to shift one's thinking, behavior, and actions to enable the innovation itself to be developed.

- Product/service development refers to actually taking the idea and building the end product or service.

- Discipline refers to ability to stick with something until it is completed despite the obstacles that get in the way.

- Product/service management refers to the ongoing management and maintenance of the new innovation.

The building blocks of corporate entrepreneurship need to be integrated into the entrepreneurial experience because they represent some of the challenges to successfully implementing it. Creativity involves heuristics, thinking and cognitive styles not used widely in business. Innovation challenges many of the basic principles of management, traditional ways of thinking and doing. The management of change is one of the most underdeveloped skills among managers.

Understanding how these building blocks interrelate is important to understanding some of the dynamics behind corporate entrepreneurship.

What ways do you encourage creativity and innovation?

_____

How easily does your organization change?

_____

1.8 Hitting the Target—*Execution*

Execution is an integral part of every aspect of corporate entrepreneuring from idea generation to implementation. It is not just an endpoint but the ongoing delivery of business value once the product, service, or business is delivered. Although there is a lot of press about the growing need to improve execution, there is a corollary need to better understand the elements that impact execution. Execution consists of a complex set of independent variables that must be factored into the equation. *Hitting the target* is only part of the equation.

Execution refers to the ability to follow through on commitments to achieve the business results intended. It includes working within certain time parameters and within budget constraints. Managing execution is only one aspect; getting the business benefits is just as important. You can deliver a project on time and on budget, but if it does not deliver the quality or intended business benefits then it has not been successful.

According to the Standish Group, in 2002 only 28% of all technology related projects were delivered on time, on budget, with the intended results. Stage gating and project management methodologies can help you improve the delivery of projects on time and on budget, but they may not help you achieve the business benefits. Benefits management refers to a process of ensuring that investments get evaluated and deployed with a solid link to benefits.

Benefits management is often a neglected aspect of new business, product or service development. Like execution, benefits management cannot be viewed as an end process but must be factored into your development process and tracked over time. There are many ways to accomplish a specific project task, but only a few that deliver benefits along the way. We'll have more on benefits management in Chapter 10.

As an entrepreneurial leader, you understand that execution is threaded throughout the development process. Each stage gate or deliverable represents an opportunity to refine the team's execution skills. Leverage these opportunities by assigning metrics and benefits where they make sense. Over time, the team will begin to see the value and importance of integrating execution and benefits throughout the project delivery process. It also helps refine their execution skills and capabilities. This will be important when the pressure is on to deliver the final project.

The successful execution of a new initiative is influenced by a number of factors. These factors include the external market, changes in technology development, organizational issues and resource constraints. Having the right target is just as important as hitting the target. As market conditions change and new competitors emerge, the realities of a new business opportunity may diminish. Leveraging or developing new technology creates uncertainties and cannot be anticipated in advance. A shift in organizational priorities, financial pressures, or a loss of a key employee can impact progress. Resource constraints are always looming, but if resources are not available when expected or reallocated to higher-priority work, they will impact your ability to execute.

Execution is also influenced by the mindset, infrastructure, processes, and people involved. Execution is a discipline that should be a strategic priority in your organization. If your organization has not established execution as a strategic priority then you might want to establish it as one of yours. Execution requires systems and processes that support it. Barriers to execution need to be eliminated and new processes need to be in place to support it. Execution is a core competency of corporate entrepreneurs. The people involved will need to have the skills, capabilities, and tools to be effective.

Establishing execution as a core competency and putting the processes in place to integrate it into the development process will enable you to measure and track progress along the way.

How effective is your organization when it comes to execution?

_____

Is benefits management an integral part of your development process?

_____

SUMMARY: Chapter 1: Explore the Next Frontier—*Corporate Entrepreneuring*

Corporate entrepreneurship is a business process that can be used to build the organization's capabilities to generate business growth. Corporate entrepreneurship transcends every aspect of the corporation and requires a major shift in orientation. Existing systems, policies, and procedures create barriers that must be dealt with. People and culture get in the way. Some of the key impediments to corporate entrepreneurship include resistance to change, lack of commitment, short-term focus, and funding. Corporate entrepreneurship challenges the very foundation of the core business and requires transforming the way the business currently operates.

The concepts behind corporate entrepreneurship are not well understood, and there is a lack of a clear definition of corporate entrepreneurship. There is also limited information about what organizational models and operating practices work best for corporate entrepreneurship. Corporate entrepreneurship is a complex process that will be different in each organization. It varies by the type of initiative, whether it is incremental or radical innovation. It requires different resources and processes depending on the type of initiative: new business, new product/service, or new process. In turn, organizations that have developed corporate entrepreneurship as a core competency have statistically performed better.

The challenge is creating the entrepreneurial mindset and infrastructure for success. This includes having the right people and processes in place to enable the organization to make the transition. Creating an entrepreneurial mindset and infrastructure is something that individuals can learn, but they must integrate it into their work. It will evolve as you move forward. Along the way you will encounter organizational obstacles and roadblocks. Determine which processes are likely to get in the way. Be prepared to deal with them as you bump up against them.

Corporate entrepreneurs are the engines of growth. They are the change agents, the independent thinkers who are motivated by a challenge. They are eager to step up and get involved. They realize that the value is in the experience and they are willing to put their job on the line to learn and grow. Entrepreneurial leaders have a broad and deep experience base that enables them to deal with uncertainty and the unknown. They can turn ideas into profitable businesses and they are willing to do whatever it takes to accomplish their task.

The building blocks of corporate entrepreneurship are rooted in creativity, innovation, and change. These three disciplines operate independently and together to turn ideas into revenue-generating businesses. They are the foundation for generating ideas, integrating them into new products and services, and making the changes necessary to move the project forward. There are millions of good ideas, but only a handful of successful ones. The challenge is finding the ideas that have business value and building the skills that enable the organization to implement those ideas. Building execution as a core competency is necessary to ensure that your best ideas get to market.

Corporate entrepreneurship sets the stage for business growth, while building an entrepreneurial framework creates the operating environment where growth can happen.

Corporate Entrepreneur Insights and Lessons Learned

- Champion—"You need a champion who is visionary and entrepreneurial."

- Entrepreneurial Leader—"Our CEO was a corporate entrepreneur. He was an innovator who was willing to take financial risks for longer-term gains. Even though we took a loss in the short term, we made it up in the long term."

- Commitment—"You need a strong commitment and ongoing support from senior management to see things through until the end."

- Political Clout—"You need political clout to keep a project like this going."

- Right Environment—"The right environment for corporate entrepreneurship includes funding, freedom, top management support and a global agenda. The company must have the appetite for this type of process for it to be successful."

- Fuse too Short—"The pocketbook was too shallow for what we were doing. The company was looking at this project as an expense, not an investment."

- Arena of Uncertainty—"There is inherent risk in corporate ventures. You are dealing with the abstract. You are operating in an arena of uncertainty."

- Complexity—"We all underestimated the complexity of building this business."

- Explorer—"Corporate entrepreneurs are never satisfied with the most obvious solution. They are always looking for another, better way that provides greater value."

- Meaning—"They were all knowledge workers looking for meaning, wanting to make a difference, recognizing that they were the future, all seeking to be true to themselves."

- Talent Magnet—"The innovation center was a symbol of change, a talent magnet attracting people who value a creative agenda. Innovation creates a venue for attracting highly creative and entrepreneurial talent."

- Change Agenda—"Our CEO made it clear that the train was leaving the station and that the company was going to change. His commitment and the support of senior management were critical for paving the way to making the change happen. It reinforced our mission."

- Success—"Nothing breeds success like success."

Chapter 2

Navigating Obstacles

Entrepreneurial Framework

Corporate Entrepreneur Insights and Lessons Learned

2.1 Big Picture

Understanding the interrelationship between corporate entrepreneurship as a business process and innovation as the successful integration of new ideas into products, services, and businesses will help you understand part of the reasons some innovations succeed, while others fail. Corporate entrepreneurship provides the framework for innovation: the people, processes, and infrastructure to support it. Innovation refers to integration of new ideas into products, services, businesses, or processes. *Establishing innovation as a strategic priority is only the first step.*

The rapid pace of change is greater than ever. Companies find that they must change just to maintain their competitive position. This is forcing companies to make fundamental shifts in the way they do business. The challenge is adapting the core business to those characteristics that are more in alignment with entrepreneurial firms. Corporate entrepreneurship is a unifying framework that enables the organization to transition to a more entrepreneurial orientation.

At the same time, many of these organizations are flush with cash and getting pressure from stakeholders to invest in new growth opportunities. Innovation is seen as the answer to the growth problem. Even though innovation has become an integral part of many strategic plans, the framework has not always been in place to support it from an operational perspective. Although there is an increase in spending on innovation, very few products or services ever get to market. The failure rate continues to be high.

You will find that focusing on innovation alone is not enough. It requires embracing the principles and processes behind corporate entrepreneurship. Organizations that jump into innovation without the entrepreneurial mindset and infrastructure in place to support it find it tough going.

Defining what innovation is for your organization is the second step. Unfortunately, organizations often narrowly define what they mean by innovation so that it looks like business as usual with a new twist. Most new products and services are retreads of existing products. You will want to determine what type of innovation is right for your organization: new to world, new to market, new product-services, product-service revisions, product-service line extension, etc.

Incremental innovation is fine for small growth goals but insufficient for stretch goals. Deciding on a mix of incremental and radical innovation over various time horizons is better. Each type of innovation has various characteristics associated with it: level of risk, investment required, return on investment, number of people involved, research requirements, development life cycle, management controls and market longevity. You will want to factor all of these into your thinking.

A key aspect of innovation is establishing the ground rules for identifying and selecting new investments. This includes defining the selection criteria, setting priorities, financial metrics, and business benefits. It also means creating thresholds for determining when investments need to be shut down. These are some of the parameters that will assist you in creating an investment portfolio for new innovations.

Decisions regarding resources and the allocation of additional funding should be evaluated in terms of the total investment portfolio and product/service priorities. There will never be enough resources to go around, so creating a process for allocating resources and funds ensures that high-priority, high-potential initiatives are preserved.

Management practices that support innovation will need to be created. Innovation challenges many of the existing management practices and control systems. Many of the traditional approaches to business will no longer apply.

You must create a change management process and develop a change agenda that makes sense. If you try to change too many things too quickly, you create greater chaos and utter confusion. Change management programs are important at both the project and organizational levels.

Another key is ensuring that you have entrepreneurial role models at the top who have the breadth and depth of experience required to see things through to completion. Employees will need to be given a level of autonomy and control that never existed before. Funding for training and development programs will be required to build entrepreneurial skills.

Create a culture that fosters new ideas for innovation. Establish a central repository for ideas and a mechanism for evaluating which ones are worth pursuing. Then make investments in those ideas that meet your threshold for success as a way to test the waters and capture learning from the experience.

The Corporate Entrepreneuring Audit™ looks at current business processes across functions to determine which ones are in alignment with the new initiative and which ones are not. It will help you identify which ones are likely to get in the way, which ones need to be tweaked or change—starting with strategy.

Operating Framework

Corporate Entrepreneuring Audit™							
Barriers to Success	Strategy	Structure	Systems	Policies Procedures	Culture	People	Customers
Performance Metrics							
Outcomes							

If you want to institutionalize entrepreneurship in your organization, you will want to integrate the following things in your strategic plans:

- Leadership—CEO is the primary driver of innovation

- Mission—innovation is part of your vision and mission statement

- Strategy—defining innovation as critical to long-term success

- Definition—articulating what types of innovation are important

- Core Competency—stated goal to develop innovation as a core competency

- Idea Management—having formal programs for idea generation/problem solving

- Alignment—clear objectives, tactics and commitment to innovation

- Role Models—identifying and developing entrepreneurial role models at the top

- Change Management—change initiative in place to support innovation

- Venture Fund—separate investment fund for innovation

- R&D—increasing levels of investment in R&D

Institutionalizing innovation is a long-term commitment in an era that has a very short-term focus. It requires a genuine commitment from the top, sufficient time for experimentation, and tolerance for failure. It requires changing the very systems, processes, and people that support the core business. It means learning from your failures and integrating your learning into new development efforts. It involves looking at the existing organization in a new light and transforming the way you do business.

Is innovation a strategic priority in your organization?

_____

Does your organization have criteria for selecting and killing new initiatives?

_____

What processes are in place to allocate resources?

_____

How are new business initiatives funded?

_____

2.2 In You We Trust

As you transform your organization to be more entrepreneurial, you will find that trust and risk are woven throughout the process. Trust in leadership is becoming increasingly important as organizations deal with the rapid pace of change. Trust between the leader and team lays the foundation for risk taking. Trust between the leader and the rest of the organization provides the framework for collaboration. Trust between the leader and senior management helps accelerate the transformation. Ultimately it is the *trust in the leader* that is often the key to success.

Trust is an integral part of leadership. As an entrepreneurial leader, you will have to navigate through uncharted waters and make unpopular decisions to keep things moving. There will be tradeoffs on the best way to use resources and allocate limited funds. You will have to take hard stands on issues that may be unpopular with the team and the organization. You will need to motivate and encourage individuals to stretch outside their comfort zone. You will ask the team to make commitments that are above and beyond the normal call of duty. As you build a stronger relationship with your team, you will come to realize that trust and risk are intertwined.

Many organizational transformations are met with a certain level of skepticism in the beginning. People prefer to wait until they see value before they are willing to lend their support. They are often more comfortable putting their trust in doing things the old way. As the leader, it will be incumbent upon you to build trust. You may find that you have to build that trust one person at a time. Having the ability to develop effective working relationships with those around you is a key component of building trust. It is all about relationship building and collaboration. As others begin to understand and see the value in what you are doing, then their trust in you will grow.

Trust between the leader and senior management is critical. Building trust with senior management will be crucial in moving things forward and getting the support you need when unpopular decisions must be made. Trust is a double-edged sword that cuts both ways. There will be plenty of opportunities for you to test your trust in one another. Senior management will not always be comfortable with your decisions but they will demonstrate their trust by delegating risk when it is required. The question is whether they will be willing to accept the results of those decisions when they don't go according to plan.

As your trust grows, so does your confidence in taking bigger, bolder risks. So it is imperative that you have the self-confidence and conviction upfront to see things through until the end. You will need to be proactive, organized, disciplined, and decisive. It will be important that you are political savvy and operate from an internal locus of control. You will need influence and good communication skills. These are the characteristics that will help you build the trust you need. Building trust will help you convince some of your skeptics, but not all of them.

As the leader you will never get the full trust of those around you. The team will present a united front to the rest of the organization, but may question you behind closed doors. You will need to build that trust. In turn, you will want the team to develop trust in themselves. Over time you will be able to determine their level of trust through their work when they stop delegating the risky decisions to you. More importantly, you will know that they have developed a level of trust in themselves to take on greater risk.

Even though your peers may lend their support, they are not always totally supportive. It is not until they are willing to put some skin in the game that you can measure their trust. There are competitive forces at work here that transcend trust. Everyone is competing for limited funding and resources. So it is not surprising that perhaps the greatest resistance you will encounter will be from your peers. You should not expect them to trust you.

It may be easier to understand the level of trust you've built with senior management. You will see it more clearly when there is a high-risk decision to be made or a major departure from normal operating procedures. Although they may have promised their support and encouragement in the beginning, it is not until you reach a pivotal point in the project that you understand their risk profile. Only then will you understand the level of trust they place in you.

Finding a leader people trust is only a small part of the challenge you face. The shortage of entrepreneurial role models at the top of many organizations is a big problem. The skills and capabilities of an entrepreneurial leader differ from those of more traditional leaders. The challenge is identifying and developing leaders who have the right combination of competencies.

Leaders will not only be judged on how well they executed, but how effectively they led. Developing entrepreneurial leaders will be your organization's greatest achievement as you build its capability to achieve business growth.

Who are the entrepreneurial leaders in your organization?

_____

What is it about their leadership style that people trust?

_____

What programs are in place to develop more entrepreneurial leaders?

_____

2.3 Importance of Circles

The circle is the universal symbol for inclusion and wholeness. Circles have no sharp edges, no hierarchy, no layers or spans of control. Circles can contract and expand as needed. They provide a context for exploration and discovery. They represent freedom of movement and promote the free flow of communication. They create an environment that fosters teamwork. Creating an organization of interlocking circles minimizes the traditional issues regarding hierarchy and control. *Structures are rigid, organizing in circles is better.*

Traditional organizational structures get in the way of new business initiatives. They were designed and developed to serve the needs of the core business, not new initiatives. Even matrix organizations get in the way. Boundaries of any kind, real or imagined, impose limits and slow things down. Positional power can get in the way as teams are more likely to defer to those in higher authority. Functional groups with more clout can wield influence. All of these elements serve to create barriers to progress. Eliminating as many of these as possible up-front levels the playing field and gets everyone working in unison.

You want an organizational design that facilitates speed and agility. Of course, this will depend on the type of initiative you are working on. A circle is just a different construct to shift your thinking about the various ways you can organize your initiative.

With an entrepreneurial start-up, you will want to be nimble and may want to start with an informal, loose structure. You will want fewer layers and a broader span of control. You will want to ensure the free flow of communication. Ideas should be bottom up, not top down. You will need adequate control systems to get started, as well as cross-functional interaction and cooperation. Management styles will be less formal and more collaborative. Teams will be empowered. As the project evolves, so will the structure.

Organizing in circles is one way to structure a new initiative. It helps eliminate some of the barriers created by traditional organizational structures. It also provides a platform for change. Every circle can represent a major function or task of a business initiative. Each of the interlocking circles is dependent on the others to accomplish the overall project. Circles must work together to achieve certain milestones and tasks. Team members can work independently on their specific tasks, but must work in collaboration with the adjacent circles to achieve all of their goals.

One entrepreneurial leader had a team of extremely bright, competitive individuals who had climbed the corporate ladder by being outstanding individual contributors. They had worked most of their careers in hierarchical organizations and were more likely to use positional power to get things done. It was clear that this type of behavior would get in the way. The leader wanted to level the playing field, so he asked the team to design a structure of interlocking circles to support all the required activities. The team divided all the work into six functional groups and outlined tasks for each group, with dependencies and interdependencies. They designed the structure and agreed to work within it until it no longer worked. They used it as the initial structure to get the project going. Of course the structure changed over time, but so did their appreciation for working as a team.

Operating Framework

Corporate Entrepreneuring Audit™							
Barriers to Success	Strategy	Structure	Systems	Policies Procedures	Culture	People	Customers
Performance Metrics							
Outcomes							

Changing structures helps shift thinking and behaviors. If you want to change the way the team works, you must set the context for that change. Changing organizational structures forces them to change. If the team can no longer rely on the traditional ways of doing things, they will have to think of new ways to get the work done. Changing structures redistributes power. Positional power is eliminated. Control is distributed to the team, creating the need for cooperation and collaboration.

It really doesn't matter what the structure looks like. You must decide what you need to change and then provide the structure for that change. It may be counter-intuitive for you to organize a major project into circles, but it forces people to approach a new initiative with a better understanding of the interdependencies.

What type of organizational structure do you use for new initiatives?

_____

What level of collaboration exists between different organizational functions?

_____

Can you imagine organizing your next big project with interlocking circles?

_____

2.4 Your Best Friends

It will not take long for you to realize that members of the finance department will quickly be *your best friends*. You will find that having financial acumen is a key component of your job, so if you are not financially savvy then it would be wise to befriend your finance people. Because it is easy for a project to quickly run into financial roadblocks, having a good handle on the finances is imperative—and who better than finance to do that with you? They understand the nuances of the financial reporting system and can help you identify potential pitfalls before they occur.

Many organizational budgeting systems do not provide adequate provisions for budgeting entrepreneurial initiatives. There is often an arbitrary allocation of costs to the new venture or the same overhead is allocated across existing operations. Not fair, you say? Well, yes and no. Yes, in that it handicaps your project from the get-go, but no because there have to be some guidelines. Inflexible budgeting systems and arbitrary cost allocations can create a burden from the start. The key is setting up a budgeting system that takes into consideration the various stages of a start-up and recognizing the burden overhead may pose while you are still doing development.

If your organization has an incubator or internal venture group, these initiatives are usually funded and managed separately. It is likely that there are already systems in place to handle financial reporting requirements. If funding is coming from multiple sources, then you may have to establish new reporting procedures. If funding is coming out of traditional budgets, then tracking and measuring performance against organizational standards creates an inherent disadvantage for the entrepreneurial initiative. These are all concerns to address before you get started.

Effective financial management of limited budgets may help you when you need to secure additional funding or reset expectations about what is actually feasible with the budget you now have. Some organizations will provide enough funding to validate the worthiness of a project. Then it is up to the team to secure additional funding for full development. Others will seed small ideas as a way to test the water with minimal risk. Either way, there is never enough to go around.

Getting funding is only the first step. Keeping that funding can be another. It isn't unusual for funds to be reallocated in midstream. Budget constraints are a normal part of doing business. Setting an expectation upfront that current budgets are soft can help you manage the funds you have more effectively. There is often a higher risk that budgets will be pulled from new initiatives. You will have to be creative with the funds you have.

Secure funding for proper incentives and spiffs. You will want to reward performance and motivate your team throughout the process. Even a small financial incentive can provide a big boost in moral and productivity. The more unexpected it is, the more appreciated it will be.

Secure funding for outside consultants, executive coaching, and team building. These things may seem frivolous but they are not. Unexpected issues will surface that no one in your organization will be able to deal with, forcing you to go outside. Having an executive coach will help you keep your sanity at the point when you think you've lost your mind.

Financial obstacles that may seem insurmountable can often be dealt with by someone who knows the details behind the numbers. Although financial reporting plays a big part in what the finance department can do for you, they provide valuable insight into better ways for you to manage the limited funds you have.

So make finance an integral part of your team. Keep them actively engaged on the project, not just when it is time to report on the financial status of the project. Make them a part of your team and integrate them into the planning process and development efforts. These individuals provide a structured view of the world that is often missing. They can also come up with creative ideas that may not be related directly to their job function.

In one company, the finance people came up with a pricing model that far surpassed anything the team was able to develop. It served to support the product pricing effort and gave the field sales force a tool to price the product with clients. It also showed the team how they could generate more revenue at the front end of a sale and over time.

Financial acumen is a must-have when it comes to new ventures. Be sure you have the skills or that someone on your team does.

How actively involved is your finance department with new initiatives?

_____

Is the finance department viewed as a roadblock or ally?

_____

Do you have a separate budgeting system for new initiatives?

2.5 Shifting Gears

There is still a limited understanding of the type of environment in which corporate entrepreneurship flourishes. Little is known about what type of corporate entrepreneurship is best under various structures, control systems, cultures and other managerial variables. Corporate entrepreneurship challenges many of the preexisting systems and processes and involves radically changing traditional forms of behavior. It creates a new set of challenges that require you *to shift gears.*

Although organizational systems create obstacles and barriers for new investment initiatives, they also provide a framework for more effectively managing them, giving them a chance to survive and thrive. Systems have been established to create order and discipline and that is what you will need. They need to be fine-tuned to reflect the reality of your particular project.

- Business Program Management

- Portfolio Management

- Risk Management

- Project Management

- Product Development

- Communications

- Technology

- Partnership Management

The need for strong project management capabilities is well understood by most organizations but applying them to large investment projects is not. *Business program management* is a management framework that provides the business oversight required to ensure success, reduce risk, and achieve the intended business benefits. It is usually used with initiatives that are high risk and will significantly impact the organization's financials. The concept is intended for directors and business unit managers assigned responsibility for managing strategic projects and mobilizing programs and projects. It is designed to provide the business management discipline that is often missing from new investments.

Business program management is an organizational practice designed to optimize the benefits flowing from an organization's investment initiatives. It is an umbrella under which the following management practices fall: strategic alignment, investment selection, portfolio management, risk management, contract management, change management, benefits management and partnership management. A business program management office is an organizational entity established to oversee all these activities.

Unlike business program management, *portfolio management* is standard practice for many organizations. Managing investment funds as a portfolio helps establish guidelines and criteria for distributing funds among new investments. It provides a baseline for developing investment guidelines for new initiatives: objectives, selection criteria, resource planning, risk management, and performance management. It also helps facilitate the allocation of scarce resources among competitive projects.

Using a formal portfolio management process enables organizations to more effectively manage new investment projects over time. Establishing a portfolio of short-, medium—and long-term product and service investments will provide the infrastructure for building a pipeline of investment opportunities. If your organization uses a portfolio management system for new investments, then it is wise to use it. You will want to understand your organization's portfolio management system and how the decision process could impact your own project.

The business case for new initiatives should be evaluated against an *investment criteria* established specifically for innovation projects. Adhering to traditional investment hurdles can handicap the project or may even prevent some good ideas from getting funding at all. Setting unrealistic financial goals from the beginning only serves to dampen the team's enthusiasm and motivation. If it takes nine months to build a new service, having a goal of profitability the first year may be totally unrealistic. Establishing a reasonable investment criteria and setting realistic goals becomes a bigger motivating factor to drive higher performance.

Managing financial risks associated with your new initiative and their impact on financial results is critical. If your organization has a *risk management* process it is important to understand how it works and where your project fits. You should have a clear understanding of the financial, technical, market, and organizational risks associated with your project. As the project evolves, the parameters for risk will change. You will need to factor these risks into your plans.

Project management discipline has become a core competency in many product-oriented industries, less so in service-based organizations. The Project Management Institute (PMI) has developed a set of project guidelines and practices that many organizations use to manage IT-related projects. Organizations will hire PMI-certified candidates to leverage this expertise. Having project standards is extremely valuable for keeping projects on track. However, standards can also be cumbersome and get in the way. Utilizing some of the fundamentals of project management makes sense. You may want to understand your organization's project management capabilities and how they can support your effort.

Most companies have standard *product development* processes in place that have evolved over time. These standard processes have helped reduce the product development cycle and time to launch. Iterative development practices have served to increase the value for customers. Stage gating has been adopted as an effective way to streamline and control the development process. Select those processes that make sense and disregard those that don't. Establish hard metrics, leave room for integrating changes as new information becomes available, and get management actively involved at critical decision points.

Communication plans provide a platform for the timely dissemination of information, effective decision making and ensuring the flow of information to the right sources. Although communication is a topic that is widely discussed in the management literature, there are many organizations that do not set up communication support systems for major investment projects. They will develop communication plans at the project level, less so up or across organizational boundaries. Communication plans should be in place for all stakeholders.

Ensuring that you have the *technology* and *technical resources* to support your initiative seems simple but it is not. The greatest challenge you may face is translating customer requirements into technical plans. Although you think the technology group gets it, assume they don't. If you think you know what you want, assume that you only know *part* of what you want. As you gather information, your needs will change and impact both development and delivery schedules. Change management practices should be used to control change requests. Tradeoffs must be made. The final product may not look anything like you envisioned in the beginning. This will drive the technology group crazy.

Dedicated resources are best, but shared resources may be all that you get. Development systems are one thing to consider, availability of systems for demonstration purposes is another. Control of resources is a variable that is often a problem. Resources outside of your control are harder to manage and hold accountable. Assigning a project manager from business and technology to own joint milestones and deliverables helps mitigate this. Establishing a partnership with your counterpart in the technology group makes it easier. Expect the unexpected and then you won't be surprised. Technical problems never surface until you least expect them.

Partnership management can be a critical piece of the puzzle. Check to see if your organization has developed partnership management processes. They can help you expedite the negotiation and contracting process with potential business, technology and outsourcing partners. Understanding the ground rules up front can save you time in identifying potential partners and head aches later in dealing with disputes. Clarify what each party brings to the table and detail that information in a partnership agreement. Decide how decisions will be made, who will be involved, and how disagreements will be resolved. It may take time up front, but it will save you time down the road.

Operating Framework

Corporate Entrepreneuring Audit™							
Barriers to Success	Strategy	Structure	Systems	Policies Procedures	Culture	People	Customers
Performance Metrics							
Outcomes							

All of these organizational systems provide value, structure, discipline, and control. They have evolved over time but are rooted in the same fundamentals that are required to support new investment initiatives. Leveraging the fundamentals behind these systems is what you will need to do. Shifting to a lower gear, a simpler version of all of these processes, will enable you to adhere to good management practices without having to burden your project.

What management systems do you use to support corporate entrepreneurship?

_____

Which management systems will you need?

_____

How will they need to be changed to support your project?

_____

2.6 Obstacle Course

Navigating your way through corporate entrepreneurship is a little like going through an obstacle course. On the first pass you won't know what to expect until you encounter it. On the second pass, you will be better prepared to deal with it and may even plan for it. On the third pass, you will discover that there are alternative ways of dealing with the obstacle in front of you. Some of the obstacles you will encounter can be identified before you get started, but others will only become visible as you make your way _through the obstacle course._

A key concern among executives is that they don't feel they have the skills or capabilities to successfully navigate their way to new business growth. There is an inherent concern about the risk and high failure rate of new initiatives. Combine this with the pressure to deliver short-term results and you can see why senior management is reluctant to take the plunge into corporate entrepreneurship. These are some of the obstacles that are at the surface. Under all of this are the hidden barriers and obstacles: the very same policies, procedures, systems, and support infrastructure that are the foundation of the core business. Tampering with some of these will rock the very foundation of the business.

Traditional management practices often have adverse effects on a new initiative. Long complex approval cycles, adhering to standard performance metrics, inappropriate incentive systems, established documentation processes, and reporting requirements are only a few. All of these are management practices that can be tweaked or changed to support new initiatives.

The following is a checklist of some of the key policies and procedures you will want to consider as you move forward:

- Performance Metrics

- Decision-Making Practices

- Approval Processes

- Incentive Systems

- Benefits Tracking

- Reporting Processes

- Cross-Organizational Collaboration

- Knowledge Capture

You need policies, and procedures in place to ensure order and maintain efficiency. This is great for the core business but gets in the way of new initiatives. They slow progress, bog down decision-making, and impact the efficiency with which you operate. There are thousands of rules, regulations, documents, policies, and procedures that you will have to deal with. Knowing up front which ones will impact you the most will be helpful; you will discover the rest along the way.

The Corporate Entrepreneuring Audit™ is a good starting point for identifying which policies and procedures are likely to get in the way.

Operating Framework

Corporate Entrepreneuring Audit™						
Barriers to Success	Strategy	Structure	Systems	Policies Procedures	Culture	People	Customers
Performance Metrics							
Outcomes							

The audit can be used as a guide to help you build the operating model that you will need to support your new initiative.

It is often a matter of control. The degree of control versus the level of autonomy is one that the company will have to decide. It is dependent on where the new initiative resides in the company. You can have projects that are centralized in R&D, developed in an incubator, or developed within a line of business. Aspects of control may depend on the type of initiative, whether it is at the idea stage, in a portfolio of high-potential opportunities or designated as a formal development effort. Each of these types of initiatives has different characteristics in terms of financing, approval process, standard processes, leadership, length of development, and expected outcomes. There can be unexpected issues like mainstreaming a new initiative back into the core business.

A major financial institution in New York established an incubator group to develop new retail banking services. The incubator group was separately funded and worked independently of the business lines. The group created new products and beta tested them with the bank's customers. Once a product was validated in the market and met the financial performance requirements, it was ready to be integrated into the core business. The problem was that the line of business was reluctant to accept the new product offerings given what they already had on their plate. No provisions had been made for mainstreaming the new products coming out of the incubator.

The goal is to provide the right balance of control and autonomy. You may not know which particular policies and practices will impact the project until you encounter them as an obstacle.

What types of controls are placed to manage new initiatives?

_____

What management practices get in the way?

_____

What policies and practices need to be tweaked or changed?

_____

2.7 See the Change

As an entrepreneurial leader, you soon come to understand why culture is often the biggest obstacle to creating an entrepreneurial venture inside an existing business. Culture is the social fabric of an organization, its personality, its values, norms, behaviors, rituals and beliefs. Like a human personality, it has evolved over time and is not easily changed. Creating an entrepreneurial culture is hard work and it will be met with resistance by those most heavily invested in protecting the status quo. Change will be slow and painful. You will wonder if it is even possible to do what you have set out to do. It will test the very essence of who you are. *You will be creating a new culture as you go.*

Culture is a powerful force that shapes our individual and collective behavior. It influences everything we do and puts limits on our thinking and behavior. It sets the tone for how we work and how we relate to others in the organization. It is a reflection of our identity, our status and power. Changing these things is difficult and scary. But change them you must.

Creating an environment for change begins with setting the stage for change. It starts with a CEO who has a propensity for change. It requires a business sponsor committed to the project and willing to stick with it despite political obstacles. It will take an entrepreneurial leader who thrives in an environment of change. It will mean building a high-performance team that can stick with it.

Embed change in the process by building a team that is a mix of individuals from inside and outside the organization. If you are not lucky enough to hire from the outside, work with outside consultants who can help you develop the necessary behaviors and team dynamics. Develop values that encourage and support entrepreneurial behavior. Establish new norms and rituals with the team. It is often the "unlearning" part of change that is the most difficult.

Be prepared to deal with ambiguity, uncertainty, and failure. If your organization is not willing or able to effectively manage these, then *you* will have to. Living with ambiguity is part of the process. Dealing with uncertainty is a daily event, and failure is always a possibility. These are core characteristics of an entrepreneurial culture and will become part of the culture you create. Learning to manage them is what will be important. Capture the lessons you learn and share them with the group. They help shape and mold future decisions.

Value and acknowledge entrepreneurship as a core competency. Provide the training and development necessary to embed these competencies into daily work practices. Establish execution as a core competency and develop execution skills as the project progresses.

Operating Framework

Corporate Entrepreneuring Audit™							
Barriers to Success	Strategy	Structure	Systems	Policies Procedures	Culture	People	Customers
Performance Metrics							
Outcomes							

Over time, the vestiges of the old culture will quietly slip away and a new culture will emerge. It is not an event but a process that is created through the collective efforts of the group. It is all about changing behaviors. It is a bonding experience that occurs because of a common vision and belief in achieving the end result. It is subtle and quiet, but it is extremely powerful.

The collective efforts of the group will shape and create a new culture. The team will begin to slowly move away from the core business and establish its own identity. The team will assert their independence and establish eminent domain. This will be threatening to the rest of the organization, which will interpret the behavior as a shift in power. Senior management will sit on the sidelines and observe this process as if it were some kind of scientific experiment. They may even question what they have created.

Change is an emotional experience and creating a new culture is a daunting task. Often this new culture is as temporary as the project that spawns it. If not, it must coexist with the core business and be an enabler for other entrepreneurial initiatives.

Does your organization have a change agenda for innovation?

Is entrepreneurship a core competency?

What processes are in place to create an entrepreneurial culture?

_____

Does your organization have a tolerance for failure?

_____

2.8 Champions of Change

Corporate entrepreneurs are change agents, individuals interested in pushing the edge of the envelope and seeing what lies beyond the organization's current boundaries. They actively seek out new opportunities to stretch and grow. They are motivated by a challenge and get bored easily. They have the energy and drive to push beyond the limits of their own capabilities. They deal effectively with ambiguity and are comfortable taking risks. They are not afraid to fail, they are restless if they don't try. Once they've accomplished a task they are eager to move on to the next opportunity. Corporate entrepreneurs are the *champions of change*.

Corporate entrepreneurs have a unique combination of skills both broad and deep. They consciously seek out opportunities to do something new, different or improved. Unlike others, they understand that the real value in what they do is in the experience itself. Despite whether they succeed or fail, it is always a win-win situation for them. Learning is a big part of who they are. You will find others who aspire to be corporate entrepreneurs. These are the individuals with a lower risk profile who are intrigued and willing to explore new opportunities only after others they trust have jumped on board. You will need both types of people on the team.

Individuals who seek out these positions prefer less formalization in terms of roles and responsibilities. They are team-based and enjoy the company of others like themselves. They are quick, deliberate and focused. They have a high self-concept and worthiness. They are competent, empathic and have an inner drive that keeps them going. You will find them more challenging to manage but more fun to work with. Their energy and enthusiasm will motivate you and keep you going when the going gets tough.

As corporate entrepreneurs gain more confidence in themselves, they will want and ask for more power. They will want more discretion in problem-solving and decision-making. You will want to encourage them to take more calculated risks.

As you feel more comfortable turning power over to them you will become more empowered yourself. Although empowerment is a term that usually refers to empowering others, you will quickly learn that the more power you give away, the more powerful you will become.

Distributing power to everyone levels the playing field and changes the rules of engagement. No longer will the team rely on you to do their bidding for them. Your people will have to develop their influencing and presentation skills. They will need to enhance their negotiation skills so they can deal effectively with conflict.

At times you will ask the team to step into your shoes and become the leader or the team builder. You will give them opportunities to interact with peers and superiors and take your place at the table. They need to experience those things that have been outside of their reach in order to stretch and grow. Traditional organizational boundaries melt away as they realize that changing the game means changing themselves.

In order to promote and develop entrepreneurial behavior, you need to encourage people to be more entrepreneurial. You will want to provide incentives and rewards for the very behaviors you are trying to develop; risk-taking, decisiveness, taking initiative, collaboration, execution and so on. You will want to make managing an entrepreneurial initiative part of an individual's career path. All of these things demonstrate the organization's commitment to establishing entrepreneurship as a core competency.

Operating Framework

Corporate Entrepreneuring Audit™							
Barriers to Success	Strategy	Structure	Systems	Policies Procedures	Culture	People	Customers
Performance Metrics							
Outcomes							

As you build entrepreneurial behavior into your culture, you will need to establish a talent management program to support it. Selection and recruiting criteria should be established. Training and development programs will be needed. As your talent pool of entrepreneurial skills grows, so will the opportunities for growth and innovation.

Can you identify the corporate entrepreneurs in your organization?

_____

What are you doing to develop and nurture these individuals?

_____

What kind of incentives and rewards are in place to encourage entrepreneurial behavior?

_____

2.9 Friend or Foe

In an ideal world you would want the human resource department to be a strong ally in your project. It really depends on the role of human resources in your organization. They can be invaluable in getting you external candidates for your project. They can help you create new incentive programs for the team. They can assist in developing the skills and competencies required for corporate entrepreneurs. Yet they can also get in the way if they do not fully understand and embrace what you are doing. *Getting support from human resources can be invaluable—or not.*

In some organizations, the human resources department or the organizational development groups think they should be leading the change initiative. If they do, it can create roadblocks for you. While a major transformation initiative will require the support and collaboration of human resources, that is not usually the case with smaller initiatives. Setting expectations upfront about how you will work with human resources will save a lot of heartache down the road.

One corporate entrepreneur had to learn the hard way. The executive in charge of human resources thought that he should be leading the change initiative because HR had led the change initiative in his previous organization. It was not surprising that he expected it in this situation, especially since the president of the division had let the HR executive believe that he would be the one driving the change effort. This caused a lot of tension and built barriers to working effectively with human resources.

The answer is not to have human resources sit on the sidelines but to get them integrated into the project early enough to make them a member of the team. Having another resource for the team is useful when it comes to hiring, dealing with personnel issues, or providing guidance about a difficult situation. If HR understands what you are doing, they can be very helpful in giving you the support and tools you need to be effective in managing the impact of change on people.

You must decide the best way to work with your human resource and organizational development groups. Identify ways they can support your efforts. Get them involved in team meetings. Allow them to understand the business objectives and what you are trying to accomplish. Enable them to establish a solid working relationship with team members, one of support and respect. They can be invaluable and are usually more than willing to help. Establishing this up front can create a win-win situation for everyone.

The human systems aspects of entrepreneurial initiatives are huge. They require a keen insight into human nature and change. You can not expect to manage all of these issues alone. Working with human resources is one solution. Working with outside consultants and coaches is another. The reality is that you will need help, and identifying the right resources in the beginning will give you resources to fall back on. Take the time to determine what works best in your organization.

As entrepreneurial initiatives grow in large organizations, there will an increasing need to find and develop entrepreneurial talent. Human resources can play a critical part in this process.

How involved is your human resource department involved in your change initiatives?

2.10 Get New Glasses

Seeing the problem through your customer's eyes is a key component of refining your innovation ideas. Relying on your customer to generate new ideas may not be. The ability to see new ideas is one thing, seeing how to make them into profitable businesses is another. Aligning customer needs with product ideas is tough. Formal concept testing processes help filter out those ideas that have merit and those that don't. Getting a clear picture of the idea and its potential may require that you *get new glasses.*

Competitive advantage is gained by getting out in front of customers and giving them something they did not know they wanted. The problem you are solving may not even exist as a problem in their mind today. Collaborating with customers in the further development of those ideas makes sense. The fragmentation of markets makes it more difficult to align specific customer needs to business ideas without understanding customer nuances. Nuances make the difference with the adoption of new ideas.

Creating a market requires due diligence that goes beyond normal market research. Even though you think you have identified and defined the product/service requirements, check again. If you've used a research company, do your own research to validate their work. It is better to take the time to do research up front than to spend time and precious resources on a project that is doomed to fail from the beginning. Leverage your sales, marketing, and customer service groups. Validate the research findings with them.

Although market research firms provide an invaluable service, they can be wrong sometimes. You may want to work in tandem with a research firm to conduct similar research and compare findings. If they match what you find, then you can feel confident that you have something worth pursuing.

In one case a technology vendor used a research firm to do preliminary research and then conducted focus groups. They used the requirements they developed to spec out the product. It was not until they were already down the road in product development that they realized that the customer requirements they had defined mapped to only one of their three target markets. Unfortunately, the requirements did not meet the specs of their primary market and required months of further development, delaying the product launch. Needless to say, they learned the lesson the hard way.

Customers should be an integral and ongoing part of your development effort. Every product idea will evolve and morph itself into something different as you move through the development process. A product concept is only as good as the picture it creates in the mind of your customer at that point in time. They will see it for what they want it to be, not what it is in your mind. Filter their perspective as you would your own.

Operating Framework

Corporate Entrepreneuring Audit™							
Barriers to Success	Strategy	Structure	Systems	Policies Procedures	Culture	People	Customers
Performance Metrics							
Outcomes							

Create an experience for your customer that integrates the idea into their thinking, and give them the opportunity to internalize its potential value in their environment. You will want to understand their markets and how your product will help them achieve their strategic objectives. It may be feasible for you to align your product development efforts with theirs. The more you embed your product into their strategy, the more successful you will be.

Leverage outside resources and consultants to test your concepts in the market and help create a market for your products. They provide another set of eyes that can provide a new perspective on the opportunity. They can be effective in validating the idea and enhancing it to better meet the needs of your target market. They will have a more realistic appreciation for its value in the marketplace. You want them to determine the reasons why it will succeed and fail. Both provide valuable insight that you may not be able to get on your own.

Aligning customer needs with new ideas requires an appropriate amount of due diligence. You will want to secure sufficient funding to do enough research to feel confident that your idea has merit and can be profitable. Even though you may know in your gut that what you are doing is right, you will need to convince others. The more clearly you see both sides of the equation, the more likely you are to align your idea with a market opportunity.

Leveraging both internal and external resources will provide the type of checks and balances that you will need to refine the idea and more closely align the idea with customers.

What steps do you take to get the right product/service requirements?

_____

How do you guarantee that your requirements are aligned with the need?

_____

2.11 Committed to an Idea

A great idea gets better if you shape it and enhance it along the way. Often the initial idea is the starting point for an even greater idea. The key is making sure that everyone fully understands the idea and stays committed to it. It is natural for senior management to get excited about the project in the beginning and lose interest over time. It is also normal for the team to shape and mold the product as it evolves. By soliciting feedback from various stakeholders and acting on them, you strengthen commitment to an idea. *Feedback and commitment move the idea forward.*

Ideas take shape in the context of a vision. Once it takes root in the hearts and minds of others, then it takes on a life of its own. Everyone will have their own interpretation of what you mean and they will see it from their specific vantage point. Each of these views is important, not only in shaping the idea but in giving you a clear understanding of what people think it is. As the idea evolves, so will people's interpretation and expectation of what it is designed to do or deliver to the organization. You will want to make sure that everyone sees the same thing.

CEO commitment to the project only goes so far. The initial euphoria can quickly be replaced by a deafening silence. Keeping your project alive in the CEO's mind will depend on his or her ability to clearly and consistently understand its longer term value to the organization. Getting him or her involved in the development of the idea will be helpful, but keeping that commitment alive and strong will be up to you.

Your sponsor will have a vested interest in keeping close tabs on your progress. Their commitment is often a reflection of what it means to them personally or professionally. Understand why this project is important to them. Make sure that you are in alignment with their interests.

The commitment of the team is grounded in something deeper. They are committed to the idea. The commitment to the idea brings them together but their own personal and professional aspirations drive them. They are looking for meaning and making a difference. They want to stretch and grow. They see it as an opportunity to do something new and exciting. Their ongoing commitment is dependent on their ability to see the project as a vehicle to help them experience those things.

Commitment from the rest of the organization is up for grabs. You will not know until you move forward. On one hand, they will have plenty of ideas about what you should do. On the other, they will be the first to dismiss the idea. Yet they can often be the ones to help you shape it into something that is more suitable for the realities of the organization and the markets it serves. Getting them to share them with you will be the best way to understand their commitment.

Get your salespeople involved from the beginning. They are on the front line and understand the customer the best. They are an excellent source of input into the idea. They are also your best critic. They have a finger on the pulse on the customer and can quickly determine if something will fly or not. They will be committed to helping you if it furthers their goals. You biggest hurdle and strongest ally will be sales. Get your support people involved because they can identify a potential issue before it arises.

Internal feedback is good, but external feedback is better. Be sure that your customers are part of your feedback loop. As the product evolves, give them an opportunity to shape it as well. Feedback and commitment go hand in hand. Integrating feedback will help shape and mold the idea into something bigger and better than first envisioned. Commitment is developed by including stakeholders in the process.

What do you do to ensure that your organization stays committed to an idea?

SUMMARY: Chapter 2: Navigating Obstacles—*Entrepreneurial Framework*

An entrepreneurial framework sets the context for business growth. It is a framework that can be used to determine which systems, processes and procedures are needed to support corporate entrepreneurship. Certain fundamental aspects of corporate entrepreneurship must be integrated into your thinking and your plans. You will encounter challenges and opportunities that you have never faced before. There will be things you may want to put in place to support you, changes you will need to consider, and obstacles you are likely to encounter. An entrepreneurial frame helps you establish the boundaries and parameters for working, which helps you deal with issues as they arise.

The current focus on innovation as a strategic priority may not be enough. Despite the focus on innovation, the results continue to be disappointing. Understanding the difference between corporate entrepreneurship as a process and innovation as the integration of ideas into products and services can help you understand why so many innovations fail to get to market. Corporate entrepreneurship helps you understand the processes required to build an entrepreneurial environment that supports innovation. There are management practices, processes, and systems that must be in place. There are necessary resources and skills, and there will be individual, team, and cultural issues to face.

The shortage of entrepreneurial role models in many organizations can impact your innovation plans. There are certain behaviors and competencies you will want in your leaders and team members. Trust will play a pivotal role—trust between the leader and the team, senior management, and key stakeholders. Traditional organizational structures can get in the way and impede progress. Designing organizational structures that support entrepreneurial behavior can increase productivity and improve performance. Aligning the team with key functions like finance and human resources can provide additional support.

Existing systems and processes will create major hurdles and obstacles to overcome. Leveraging those that support your effort will be easy, changing those that do not will be more difficult. It is not always clear what obstacles you will encounter along the way, and some organizational obstacles will not become visible until you try to navigate them. Realize that you will be creating new systems and a new culture as the project evolves. Find the individuals who thrive on change and get them to carve a new path for the others to follow. Make sure you have ongoing commitment and support from senior management, because they provide the political clout you may need some day.

An entrepreneurial framework helps you create the operating environment that corporate entrepreneurs will need to be successful.

Corporate Entrepreneur Insights and Lessons Learned

- Goals—"The new CEO championed the project because it helped him achieve his innovation goals."

- Political Capital—"In our organization, the CEO was the good cop, the project sponsor was the bad cop. The CEO gave us political capital, the sponsor a dose of reality. We needed both to keep things moving."

- Impatient—"People get impatient. They don't understand that these types of initiatives take time and patience."

- Importance of Hierarchy—"Being new to the organization, I underestimated the importance of hierarchy and how it can get in the way. We needed a more flexible organizational model to get things done."

- Anchor—"At times the organization felt like an anchor around our necks. It was easier when they gave us more room to maneuver. By lightening up on the controls, we were able to get more done."

- Stovepipes—"The bigger issue at hand was breaking down stovepipes (silos) and leveraging existing expertise in new ways, a task that even the most astute find challenging."

- Virtual Organization—"The commitment was there, but building a new business with a virtual organization made leading the effort more difficult. We did not have control over the resources nor were we able to hold people accountable. It isn't the best way to build a new business."

- Operating Model—"The existing operating model was not good for the new initiative, so we had to work around it."

- Operating Committee—"Decisions were made by the operating committee. They managed the investment portfolio. We had to present a solid case for the product because they were making tradeoffs between new investments and investing in improving operations. Despite pressure to put money back into operations, the CEO would intervene and allocate funds to new projects."

- Measurements—"The existing measurements and metrics didn't work for what we were doing. We needed to develop new measurements to track and monitor our progress."

- Setting Expectations—"We tried to set expectations up front that the average product takes 12 to 18 months and that 85 percent of new products fail. It wasn't clear if the company had a tolerance for failure, and if not, what that meant to those of us on the team if we failed."

- Failure—"It was clear from the beginning that the product would not make a profit, but the organization continued down that path. It didn't make sense. If the product is not profitable, it is a failure."

- Success and Failure—"Failure means something different to everyone. You need to define what success and failure mean in your organization."

- Uncertainty—"Given the uncertainty of the pending merger, I anchored the project in more than one business line for more security. My goal was to preserve the integrity of the project, no matter what happened. It made me realize how fragile things can be."

- Client-Focused—"Being client-focused required a lot more effort than the company was used to. We realized that we needed to check our own work, so we hired outside consultants to validate our findings before we proceeded."

- Financial Acumen—"We needed to have someone from finance work with us."

- Human Resources—"We partnered with HR to help us hire over 100 people."

- Politics—"The politics surrounding our project were huge. They extended way beyond what was visible on the surface. Politics got in the way a lot and slowed things down."

- Power—"Power and politics began to rear their ugly heads and soon became an obstacle that slowed us down."

- Political Gain—"Executives were interested in the project only if there was political gain in it for them."

- New Projects—"After a while if there was anything new on the table, you learned not to get too excited about it. There were no support systems to support these new initiatives, so very few people were willing to sign up."

- Lessons Learned—"The organization did not have a lot of experience with this type of project. We had learned a lot about what worked and what didn't, you think they would have wanted to carry those lessons forward."

- Case Study—"Our CEO put the lessons learned from our innovation center into a case study to share with the rest of the organization."

Chapter 3

Discipline to Succeed

Project Management

3.1 Equation—structure and skills are required for project management *discipline*

3.2 Playbook—establishing project *standards* up front gets everyone on the same page

3.3 Stake in the Ground—put a stake in the ground with a project *charter*

3.4 Roadmap—without a high-level work *plan,* you can get lost

3.5 Town Crier—effective *communication* is a pivotal piece of project management

3.6 Red, Yellow, Green—*reporting* progress is easier when it is visible to everyone

3.7 Rules—to expedite working together, teams must establish *rules of engagement*

3.8 Coming Up for Air—establish regularly scheduled meetings and *breaks*

3.9 Illusion of Time—its all about *execution* and watching the clock slows you down

Corporate Entrepreneur Insights and Lessons Learned

3.1 Equation

Project management is both a discipline and a strategic capability that organizations use to adapt to the rapid pace of change. Project management is often narrowly defined as planning, development, and execution when, in fact, it is much more. It is set of processes, methods, tools and techniques for embedding discipline into managing projects. It is a body of knowledge that is used to guide the development of projects to improve project performance, to better control costs, and to deliver higher business value. The integration of project management practices into projects is dependent on the skills, competencies, and experience of project managers. *Both structure and skills are required for project management discipline.*

The objective of this chapter is to highlight some of the project management tools and techniques that can help teams develop the discipline required to be more effective in building new businesses, products and processes. Although the concept of project management is well-understood, the value of project management to corporate entrepreneurship is less well-known.

The complexity, unpredictability, and risk associated with innovation projects makes applying project management discipline more challenging. There are differences in how project management is used in service-based companies versus product-based companies. Project management practices must be adapted to the type of project. Staffing requirements can vary depending on the level of complexity.

Project management methodologies provide the needed structure and discipline. They are normally used by the information technology group to guide the product development process. There are numerous project management methodologies available. If you are currently using a project management methodology, determine how well it fits. Some project management methodologies are heavy on process and actually slow things down. You need to be agile, flexible, and adaptable, but operate within some larger project parameters. Project management methodologies should serve to streamline the development process, not get in the way.

Discipline is also derived from product development processes. The best-known of these is stage gating. The stage gate model consists of a series of steps which must be successfully completed before you can proceed to the next phase. Management approval is required before the project can move through the next gate. It provides a series of checks and balances that ensure the product development process is on track. It helps organizations break large projects down into smaller pieces, and helps them identify problems earlier in the project. It is a useful process for accelerating product creation and development.

The division of a large pharmaceutical company used a stage gating process to create and deliver new product innovations to the rest of the organization. The company had recognized that in order to grow they needed to make fundamental changes in the way they developed new products. The innovation center was created to accomplish that goal. The entrepreneurial leader chosen to lead the group brought strong marketing and branding expertise. He was keenly aware of the need to bring discipline to this newly formed group. He had seen far too many products get developed that were not in alignment with customer needs.

The leader also understood the challenge of bringing together a cross-functional group of people from research and development, marketing, branding, and logistics to create brand-new products. At the time, the division had no standard product development process, so one needed to be created. The leader was familiar with the stage gate model, new types of concept testing, and different tools to validate ideas. He developed a new product development process that included everything from evaluating concepts and testing prototypes to actually defining final products. They had to sort through hundreds of product ideas to get ten good ones to test. The stage gate process provided the discipline they needed to develop and eventually launch a series of successful new products.

Using a project methodology or stage gating approach is only half of the equation. A methodology is only as good as the individuals tasked with using it. Skills, competencies, and experience are necessary to drive the project to a successful completion. Experienced project managers can make a world of difference. They know how to leverage project management practices. They know which tools and techniques will be effective in a given situation. They have the discipline required to keep projects on track and deal with the unexpected.

Project managers understand the basics behind project management. The basics can be learned but they also have to be experienced. There are a number of training courses available to project managers from major universities, training organizations, or consulting firms. Beyond this, the project managers' experience can make a real difference. There is no substitute for experience when it comes to managing large innovation projects. Individuals who think they can make decisions on the fly will quickly see how fast things can spiral out of control.

Failure to factor structure and skills into your project development process can be a recipe for disaster. The reluctance of many organizations to take the time up front to adequately set up projects is on of the reasons for the high failure rate. As painful as it may seem, putting the structure and skills in place to support your project will pay dividends in the end.

Is project management a core competency of your organization?

_____

Does your organization use a project management methodology?

_____

Does your organization use a stage gating process for product development?

_____

Do you have the skills and structured methodology to support your initiative?

_____

3.2 Playbook

Standards refer to project management practices and information used to develop and manage a project. Setting project standards defines the context for doing the project work. The intent here is to get the team to understand that they need three things moving forward: a project plan, communication plan and reporting system. A project plan is a roadmap and describes how you are going to get there from here. A communication plan is a process used for disseminating information about the project to various stakeholders. A reporting system is a mechanism for reporting financials. *Establishing these project standards helps get everyone on the same page.*

Project management practices have been adopted by the technical side of organizations for a while, but they have had a slower adoption on the business side. It is important for the business side to integrate these practices into their own thinking and operations.

An excellent resource is the Project Management Institute (PMI), a nonprofit organization that has developed a set of project management standards. These standards have evolved over time, are widely adopted, and generally accepted as best practices. PMI has also published *A Guide to the Project Management Body of Knowledge (PMBOK® Guide)*, which provides an overview of project management processes and knowledge applicable to various types of projects across industries. Although PMI is accepted as the standard, it is only a guide for you to follow and adapt to your organization.

The basics of project management are grounded in what's called the triple constraints: time, budget, and quality. Time refers to the time allocated to deliver the project. The budget refers to the costs and recourses that are available. Quality refers to the parameters that must be met for the project to be a success. Under normal conditions at least one of these is fixed, sometimes two. Tradeoffs will have to be made if any of these constraints change. Effectively managing and controlling these is important.

Triple Constraints

Implicit in this is managing risks, communicating progress, and managing scope creep.

It is not unusual for projects to get started without the proper processes in place to support it. The three key processes that can be the most useful for the business are the high-level work plan, the communication plan, and the reporting system. At a major information services company there was no project plan on the business side just IT, communications was haphazard at best and financial reporting was done formally every month. No plan meant that everyone worked on things that they felt were important. Timetables slipped and priorities and contingencies did not get managed.

A work plan describes the various phases of development and the deliverables associated with each phase of the project. Used primarily on the technical side, the business has their own set of deliverables and time lines associated with a project. The communication plan provides a uniform way to communicate the status, issues, and major accomplishments of a project. It has many levels: the team, the project sponsors, and senior management. The communication plan should be directed to the needs of each of these groups on a regular and timely schedule. You may use your organization's standard reports, but you will also want to establish other reports that convey in a more concise and clear way where you are with a project.

One of the biggest challenges will be getting everyone to adhere to standards and project processes. Even in organizations with good project management practices, it is difficult to keep everyone on task. The desire is there, but often the discipline is not. Make sure everyone is working from the same playbook.

What project management standards do you use to manage projects?

3.3 Stake in the Ground

Project management discipline starts with establishing a clear and common understanding of what the project is all about. You will want to create a document that provides a high-level overview of the project that everyone can understand and adopt. Organizations refer to this document as a project charter. This document is multi-purpose: to announce the project, establish a common understanding and set expectations with the team and all the stakeholders. It is an executive summary of the project, a formal announcement and preliminary roadmap for the project. *Put a stake in the ground with a project charter.*

The purpose of the charter is to establish that the project and project manager have been authorized to move forward with the project. In some organizations, it is used to get approval to proceed. The project charter helps establish a set of expectations and boundaries for the project. It helps the organization understand the reasons for doing the project and eliminates any concerns about what the project means to others in the organization. The team can use it as a starting point for developing more comprehensive project plans. There should be no room for doubt about what the project is intended to achieve.

The project charter is a high level summary of the project. The following document is a useful starting point for developing your own project charter:

Project Charter

Project Charter		
Project Name	Project Sponsor	Project Manager
Problem Statement or Opportunity		
Goal		
Objectives		
Success Criteria		
Assumptions and Risks		
High Level Deliverables		
Time Line	Project Start	Project Completion
Prepared By	Date	Approved By

The document begins with a statement of the problem or opportunity. The goals and objectives will help clarify what the project is intended to accomplish. The goal should be as clear and succinct as possible. The objectives provide further clarification of the goals. The success criteria should describe the measurable value that will result from doing the project, as well as the intended business benefits. The assumptions, risks, and obstacles should be outlined. These are the potential threats that can affect the project's outcome. They can include financial, technical, organizational, and market risks.

You will also want to provide a high-level overview of key deliverables and timetables. They will help set the context for the size and magnitude of the effort. Key management personnel should be identified, as well as the project sponsor. This information should be sufficient to get everyone grounded and on the same page.

The document itself should be distributed to key stakeholders and posted on the general project web site for the rest of the organization. Stakeholders include anyone who can be negatively or positively impacted by the project. Every stakeholder will have their own interpretation of what the project is all about. This document helps clarify what the project is. It is an excellent executive summary to use across organizational boundaries and with external partners. Nothing in the document should be proprietary or confidential.

You should not underestimate the importance of formally announcing a new project. The division of a major Fortune 500 company had developed the business case for developing a new business. This was one of two projects that were funded from the parent company's venture fund that year. The funding, however, was contingent on getting an experienced entrepreneurial leader on board. An individual was selected from outside the company. On his first day on the job, the new leader started talking to peers and nobody even knew why he was hired. A number of these other executives had applied for the same position, and they were totally surprised to find out that someone from the outside had been hired and that the project had been funded.

A few months later, the project leader was introduced to the CEO of the corporation. The CEO acted surprised to hear what the new person was doing. It seems that it was a surprise to everyone: employees, peers, and even the CEO. A simple one-page project charter would have helped focus everyone and gotten things off on the right foot.

A project charter also helps the team convey information about the project in a concise and clear way. You want everyone on the same page, and this is a good way to get everyone grounded.

Does your organization use project charters for new initiatives?

3.4 Roadmap

Planning is one of the most critical aspects of project management, yet it is given the least amount of attention in some organizations. Planning is a function that both the business and information technology group should be involved in together. The business is usually responsible for developing the top-down approach, and the information technology group will drive the planning from the bottom up. This plan is then used by the project manager and information technology group to develop a detailed project plan. But this is often where planning stops for the business. The business side is less likely to develop their own high-level work plan. *Without a high-level work plan, you can get lost.*

A high-level work plan helps define the approach, boundaries, resource estimates, and estimated timelines. This high-level work plan helps clarify the project parameters for the team. It helps the business understand what they are responsible for and what the information technology group is expected to do. Working in partnership with the IT group is essential. The IT group is tasked with actually developing the product, so they have a vested interest in making it successful. They want to know that you are in this together. Often they are seen as an impediment, but in reality they can be your best ally.

The IT group will be the ones who sort through the details so you don't have to. They will develop the work breakdown structure (WBS), project phases, timelines, deliverables, key tasks, and staff accountabilities. They will work around the clock to meet deadlines to meet milestones and deliverables. They will be the ones to tell you news you don't want to hear and they will be the ones who come up with alternative ways to get around issues. They will understand the implications of making changes.

In turn, you need to live up to your side of the bargain. You will want to develop a high-level work plan for the business. The IT group will want to be kept up-to-date on the status of deliverables and timetables from the business side. They will want to be made aware of any changes that may impact the project, including both internal and external factors. They will want to be involved in any major decisions that will impact the deliverables or final delivery date.

The high-level plan is designed to create a road map for the team to follow as the project moves forward. It provides the baseline process to assign, delegate and control the work. Yet it gives the team the freedom and flexibility to determine the best way to carry out the work. The chaotic nature of new business initiatives makes it more critical to manage these fundamental processes.

A major mutual fund company wanted to build a new product to expand sales into their existing client base. They had developed a solid book of business but were facing competitive pressures to expand their service offerings to retain clients. The business came up with a great new product idea and then threw it over the wall to the technology group to develop. The technology group was diligent about putting together a project plan that was realistic and met the needs of the business and their clients.

Once the plan was approved and funding was allocated, the technology group got started. Using rapid prototyping helped accelerate the product development process. The problem was that the more the business got excited about what they saw, the more they wanted. They continued to lob new requests over the wall to IT. Eventually the technology group was swimming in requests for the product that were impossible to do within budget or time constraints.

Needless to say, the project was over budget and a year behind schedule. There was no process in place between the business and IT to jointly manage the product development process. As a result, the product development effort got completely out of control, the business was upset with IT, the technology group was burnt out, and clients were upset that the firm had not kept its promise to deliver the new product. To resolve the situation, the firm decided to establish a project management office (PMO) to institute more disciplined processes between the business and IT.

Closing the gap between business and the IT group is one of the greatest challenges. Both sides need to bring discipline to the process. It is surprising what can be achieved when the business and IT both understand their roles in the project development process.

Are high-level work plans developed and used to manage the business side of projects?

3.5 Town Crier

Communication is a multi-dimensional activity that, if used effectively, can provide the ongoing support required to keep a new initiative moving forward. Keeping the new investment front and center is an ongoing task. Not only do you need to keep the lines of communication open you need to consistently keep the momentum and interest level high. Senior executives can quickly loose interest on a long term project. A communication plan can be as simple as a matrix that identifies the individuals you need to communicate with, the level of detail they require, how the information is to be presented, and how frequently. The objective is to ensure that everyone who needs to know is kept apprised of progress. *Effective communication is a pivotal piece of project management.*

In the beginning of every new initiative, there is excitement and a lot of fanfare about the idea. Senior management is actively involved in getting support from the board and selling the idea to the rest of the organization. Momentum builds as the team comes together and the resources are put in place to get things started. The initiative is formally blessed and things are off and running. But the initial excitement fades quickly. Creating a communication plan that keeps everyone informed is the best way to keep the momentum and excitement of the project alive.

A great way to get started is to have a kickoff meeting. It is a good way to announce the project and get everyone excited about what you are doing. Invite all the key players and stakeholders. Give them an overview of the project and hand out the project charter. Introduce the team and key participants. Have the CEO say a few words and ask your sponsor to talk about the importance of the project to the organization. Open the session to questions and be open to suggestions. The kickoff meeting sets the tone for the project and generates excitement for everyone involved.

Once the project is underway, you will want to ensure that your communication plans are in place. It is not only important to have a communication plan to disseminate information, it is also equally important to effectively manage communication. Until the project is firmly established, there is risk involved in sharing too much information. Too much information can have negative consequences. Determining who needs to know what and when is important.

Managing the frequency of communication is also important. Regularly scheduled briefings and updates will enable you to better manage communications flows. Review meetings need to be scheduled with the team and sponsor on a regular basis. Communication with the steering committee can be on a monthly basis. You will probably want a weekly update from the project manager. Meetings are an excellent forum for communication, but they are also time-wasters if the objectives, content, and audience are not clear.

Communication Matrix

What	Client	Project Leader	Team A	Team B	Sponsor	Steering Committee
Formal Status Reports	monthly	weekly	weekly	weekly	monthly	monthly
Team Meetings	twice month	weekly	weekly	weekly		
Status Updates	weekly	weekly	weekly	weekly	weekly	as needed
Phone Calls Emails	as needed	as needed	as needed	as needed	as needed	as needed
Project Web-site	daily	daily	daily	daily		

Establishing standard formats for presenting information makes it easier for participants to absorb and manage information over time horizons. Determining which vehicles of communication are best for which groups can save time and effort: executive briefings, formal reports, emails, PowerPoint presentations, intranet, etc.

Never assume that senior management is on top of things. A large insurance company embarked on a year-long strategic project with an initial investment of several million dollars to develop a new service. Five years later, the project was still going and the investment was more than three times the initial investment. Even though the CEO had made the request, he was no longer involved. The senior executives on the steering committee weren't clear on the end goal and the project sponsor was frustrated that the project was taking so long. The question was raised as to whether there was even a reason for continuing. It took an outside consultant to come in and sort out the situation. The client need was still there, but the window of opportunity for the service had passed.

Proactively managing communication is a key responsibility of the entrepreneurial leader. It is easy for senior management to get distracted and lose interest in something that takes six, twelve or eighteen months to deliver. The organization itself will move on to other pressing priorities, and fighting for cross-functional resources can become more difficult. The team can easily get demoralized if they believe their work is undervalued or that it has taken a back seat.

Communication plans are a key component of keeping the project front and center in the hearts and minds of your stakeholders.

Do you develop communication plans for new business initiatives?

3.6 Red, Yellow, Green

One of the more difficult and frustrating things is to understand exactly how a project is progressing. You need to create a sense of urgency and manage progress proactively. The read, yellow and green approach makes it very clear where things stand and what the issues are. Using the stoplight approach in reporting progress is an effective way to get everyone up to speed quickly. It is simple and the colors red, yellow, and green convey in an instant the status of various parts of the project. *Reporting progress is easier when it is visible to everyone.*

The stoplight approach can be used to track the status of tasks, milestones, and deliverables. Green says that everything is on track and there are no major issues. Yellow conveys caution and indicates that there may be some issues, delays, or obstacles that need to be monitored. Red indicates that things are in trouble and need immediate attention. This approach is also a subtle reminder that everyone's work will be measured and tracked, so there is no hiding.

Even though you may need to adhere to standard reporting systems, you will want to develop a reporting format that accurately highlights the status of milestones and deliverables. Standard reporting systems are often overkill for a new investment initiative. Make sure that whatever reporting mechanism you choose provides adequate information for decision-making, resource management, identifying potential risks, and financial status. Incorporate the stoplight approach into your reporting system. It is simple process that is very effective.

It is also important for the internal team to understand the dynamics and status of other parts of the project. A major project can have hundreds of people involved, which makes keeping track of everyone's progress difficult. Posting status reports on the Intranet helps keep everyone informed. This approach provides consistency across the project. Over time, you may want to create a web site for the project so various stakeholders can keep track of your progress.

Using the stoplight approach to reporting also helps convey a sense of momentum and movement, which is often lacking when team members are bogged down in daily tasks. It is easy to lose sight of how much real progress the team has actually made. Encouragement can provide an added boost when team members are lost in their work. This approach is also a subtle reminder that everyone's work will be measured and tracked.

Underlying all of this is the need to establish a process for dealing with the red and yellow items and getting things back on track. It will be helpful to establish some guidelines for dealing with both the red and yellow items. Managing these and tracking them over time will ensure that things don't get overlooked. A simple action plan will often suffice. Major or unexpected issues may require a shift of resources and funding.

The stoplight approach provides a common language that can be used to discuss project progress with all stakeholders

What techniques are you using to report on project progress?

3.7 Rules

A key aspect of discipline is making sure that everyone adheres to the same rules of conduct. Without spelling these rules out in advance, everyone is left to operate the way they normally do, good and bad. The focus of this section is establishing how teams will operate, behave and work together. Before a team dives into a project, they need to create a formal list of rules for effectively working together. This is a process to get everyone involved upfront to determine the best way to work together. The team creates a formal list of rules for effectively working together. They set the rules and they must live by them. *To expedite working together, teams must establish rules of engagement.*

Rules of engagement refer to ways individuals will work together and interact. It describes methods for communicating and conducting themselves in meetings. It deals with how disputes or disagreements will be handled and how decisions will be made. Since no two people have the same work habits or styles, it is important that the team create and agree on a list together. Then there is no backpedaling or finger-pointing when rules are stretched or broken. It is up to the team to set the rules and adhere to them.

Rules of engagement may seem small and inconsequential, yet they are key ingredients of developing disciplined project teams. Although developing and managing an innovation is a daunting task, it is often the details that get in the way and slow things down. Unproductive meetings waste time. Little things like not having meeting agendas, not taking meeting notes, not capturing action items or assigning people to them all waste a lot of time. Know which people need to be involved in meetings and which do not. All of these have a ripple effect that cumulatively can cost you precious time.

Dealing with disputes or disagreements can cause major disruptions. Getting into heated discussions or arguing wastes time. Rules are intended to set the tone for how the team will operate and how they will deal with issues, make decisions, handle disputes, and communicate. Have rules about simple things like returning phone calls or emails within a specific time frame, as well as more complex issues like resolving disputes in a timely fashion or breaking stalemates. Determine what constitutes a breach of trust or what things discussed among the team should remain within the team.

Having a clear set of roles and responsibilities is also important. Although these are not exactly rules of engagement, they are important for understanding which individuals are responsible for what parts of the project. You will want to understand the scope of their responsibilities and all the hats they are wearing as part of the project. Define the roles and responsibilities of members of the team, business analysts, IT, business sponsors, steering committee, etc.

Roles and responsibilities is an area that is often ignored. The value of defining roles and responsibilities is underestimated. A simple matrix should suffice to identify who has what role, who reports to who, what are their responsibilities, and what decisions are they authorized to make. Defined roles and responsibilities give everyone a reference point for dealing with issues as they arise. When things break down—and they inevitably *will* break down—the failure to define roles and responsibilities will get in the way, complicating communications, wasting time, and protracting dealing with the problem.

Post the rules of engagement and roles and responsibilities on bulletin boards and hand them out to team members as a reminder of their commitment to the team. If rules are broken, there must be a process for resolving situations in a timely manner. One organization had a 24-hour rule: the parties involved had to resolve the situation within 24 hours or it would be handled by the leader. Team members should be encouraged to find their own way of dealing with conflict and resolving problems among themselves.

It is also important to recognize that the rules of engagement apply to the leader. The entrepreneurial leader is also a team member. At times the leader needs to roll up his or her sleeves and actively participate in the development effort. You quickly realize that sitting on the sidelines and coaching from the cozy comfort of your office is not an option. Active participation and adherence to the established rules of engagement are the best ways to instill the same discipline in the team.

Rules of engagement simplify work processes and leave less room for interpretation. Establishing rules in the beginning provides the overarching discipline that will be required as the team moves deeper into the project

What impact will having rules of engagement have on your projects?

3.8 Coming Up for Air

A high-performing team will work endless hours focused on the task at hand, yet they often neglect taking time to surface to gain some perspective. People get so absorbed in what they are doing with all the time pressures they do not take the time to come up for air. This is what causes more stress in the situation. Sometimes you have to force people to take a break. Having regularly scheduled meetings is just one way to do that. *Establish regularly scheduled meetings and breaks.*

Holding team meetings gives members an opportunity to step back and look at what they are doing. It also gives them an opportunity to look at the situation from a new vantage point. It helps them reenergize themselves. As the leader, it is incumbent upon you to ensure that the team members take some breaks.

Regularly scheduled team meetings are good if they are kept short and to the point. There is nothing worse than sitting in a meeting when you know you have a ton of things to finish before the end of the day. Holding meetings over lunch provides an excellent forum for lively discussions and bringing people up to speed on the status of various tasks. A lunch meeting also provides a less formal way of getting people to communicate and often facilitates the flow of new ideas. The team returns to their tasks with a fresh perspective and a renewed sense of commitment to the project.

In turn, team members need to be responsible for taking time to unwind and refresh themselves. It is easy to get so wrapped up in your work that you lose sight of things that can be detrimental to your health and emotional well-being. The work can be demanding and you may think that you never have enough time to take a break, but make the time. Just walking at lunch or taking a break to clear your head is all that may be required to break the logjam. Because this is often easier said than done, you need to establish rituals that break the cycle and enable you to stop once in a while.

Every team will develop its own rituals. One team would congregate at lunch and watch 20 or 30 minutes of a movie each day. It was a nice escape and helped clear their minds of all the noisy mental chatter that can get in the way of breakthrough thinking. Another team got in the habit of driving for coffee mid-afternoon, because it provided them with time to shut down and get outside. Another diversion was the internal putting championships or Nerf basketball games that ensued.

It is also important that the rest of the organization not interpret this behavior as goofing off. Think of it as a way of letting off steam, getting your second wind, and dealing with stress. The rest of the organization will look at this bizarre behavior and wonder what's going on. It may be difficult for them to understand how the team can work so hard and still have fun, but you know that it is a vital part of keeping up the momentum and reenergizing the team.

It is important to remind everyone that taking a break is a good thing. You will inevitably work harder than you ever have before, but you will also be motivated and inspired to keep working. Getting exhausted or sick will only backfire on you.

Find your own way to come up for air. A few minutes may be all that it takes to find the answer to a tough problem or give you a new burst of energy.

What things are you doing to help the team unwind and take breaks?

3.9 Illusion of Time

Time is an illusion when you are involved in an entrepreneurial project. It is easy for time to slip away when you are involved in a project. Watching the clock can actually slow progress when you are actively engaged in a new business or product/service initiative. There is an illusion that at the beginning of each project you have time to get it done. Then when time starts passing you by you start worrying about the time not the work. Staying focused on the work is what is important not watching the clock. You don't have time to think about time. Thinking about time only slows you down. *It is all about execution and watching the clock slows you down.*

If you have six months to develop a project, you have high expectations in the beginning that you have plenty of time. By the end of the first month you ask yourself where the time went. By the third month you start to get worried that perhaps you should be further along. By the fifth month you realize that you've got thirty days left and you are almost out of time. If you focus on time, then time becomes the priority. If you focus on the work, then execution becomes your primary concern.

It is extremely difficult to determine how long a new development effort will actually take. Estimates are just that—estimates. They are often developed to meet organizational timetables that may be unrealistic or out of sync with the realities of the task at hand. Especially with new innovation initiatives, it is difficult to know how organizational roadblocks will impact timetables or if unexpected issues will arise. These are the things that are not always factored into project plans.

You will want to establish realistic timetables and follow project plans as closely as possible. But being married to a date that was a best guess at the time can either be a good guide or a distraction.

Time is an illusion. It is only when you focus on time that you lose perspective on the end game, and that's when you often *do* run out of time. Think about the work and *how* you will get it done, not *when*. You will be surprised that the work often gets done, despite the time pressures, when the team focuses on the tasks in front of them.

How does clock-watching hinder or impede the progress of projects?

_____

Is your organization focused on the end goal or tracking time?

_____

SUMMARY: Chapter 3: Discipline to Succeed—*Project Management*

Project management provides a disciplined approach for developing and delivering new products and services. It is a set of methods, tools and techniques that enable the effective initiation, development and delivery of products in a timely and cost-effective manner. It is based on a set of best practices defined by the Project

Management Institute that have been established as standard practices across a variety of industries. These practices provide the discipline that is often lacking in many entrepreneurial initiatives.

Leveraging project management practices is only half of the equation; you must also have project management skills. Experienced project managers understand the tools and techniques for integrating discipline into a project. Project management standards help get everyone working from the same playbook. Standards refer to the processes and information that can be used to streamline the development process.

A project charter is used to announce and officially launch your project. It puts everyone on notice that the project is funded and moving forward. A high-level work plan will ensure that the business and information technology groups are working in parallel to achieve their respective deliverables. Even if there is a technical plan, the business should develop a high-level work plan to follow. Keeping the project visible is a good way to keep it alive. Communication plans should be in place for all of your key stakeholders, but not everyone needs or wants to know the same level of detail. Reporting progress is easier when you keep it simple and to the point. Find ways to provide status reports that are easy to understand and quickly identify issues needing attention.

Establish rules of engagement with the group. These help you define how the team will interact. They help expedite working together and dealing with problems as they arise. Schedule regular breaks and team meetings to change work patterns and get people to step back to gain some perspective. Get people focused on the work, not on watching the clock, because clock-watching only seems to slow things down.

Project management practices can provide the team with the discipline to keep things on track.

Corporate Entrepreneur Insights and Lessons Learned

- Project Management—"Project management was a necessity for discipline."

- Planning—"We did the planning as we moved along. It was a rolling plan."

- Criteria for Success—"We needed to develop new measures for scoring and evaluating new product ideas to weed out those that were mediocre."

- Discipline—"As a financial institution, we did not have the discipline around product development, so we brought in packaged goods people who did. They helped us create the discipline we needed."

- Process Leader—"We created a process to vet all of our ideas, concepts, and products. Then we identified one individual to be the process leader. With this in place, we had the discipline we needed to look at hundreds of product ideas."

- Closing the Gap—"Having deep technical and business experience made a difference in making the product successful. We closed the gap between business and technology and delivered a highly successful product to the market."

- Service-Based Businesses—"Corporate entrepreneurship is different in services versus product businesses."

- Rapid Iterative Prototyping—"The only way we could get the product developed in the time frame allotted was to build a visual prototype, which we did within days. In parallel, we developed the detailed product requirements. This iterative approach helped us refine the product requirements and kept us on track."

- Deliverables—"Everything is harder and takes longer than you expect. We did not factor that into our plans. There was little choice but to work around the clock or be late on our deliverables."

- Time—"The team was working 60 to 80 hours a week, even working around the clock to meet deadlines."

- Accountability—"It is impossible to manage a multi-million-dollar project when the people responsible for developing the product are not held accountable for the deliverables."

- Reporting—"We had to create our own reports for reporting progress."

- Home Run—"If you hit a home run you would get another project. If you failed, you and your career were sidelined.

Chapter 4

Pioneers Chart a New Course

Corporate Entrepreneurs

4.1   Similar but Different—the small *nuances* are what set them apart

4.2   Meaning of Work—making a *difference* is what is important

4.3   Belonging—there is a human need to *belong*

4.4   Park Your Ego at Door—there is no room for *prima donnas*

4.5   Can-Do Attitude—if you *believe* you can, you can

4.6   Relying on Intuition—sometimes *intuition* will have to do

4.7   Living on the Edge—let the *momentum* of the team carry you

4.8   Weekend Warriors—the six-day *work week* is not unusual

4.9   Going Home—the experience will change your *perspective* on work

Corporate Entrepreneur Insights and Lessons Learned

4.1 Similar but Different

Corporate entrepreneurs are independent thinkers who thrive in an environment of change. They are goal-oriented, creative, decisive, aggressive, and competitive. They have a thirst for knowledge, a high tolerance for stress, and they make things happen. They are not unique, they just have a unique combination of behaviors and competencies that distinguish them from others. On the surface they appear to exhibit some of the same behaviors and competencies as traditional employees. *The small nuances are what set them apart.*

The Corporate Entrepreneur Profile™ provides insights into the critical behaviors and competencies of corporate entrepreneurs and entrepreneurial leaders. The profile was designed and developed from academic research, business journals, and corporate entrepreneurs. It was validated and tested with senior-level executives who were experienced corporate entrepreneurs and entrepreneurial leaders from several industries. Each of these individuals had extensive experience building new growth initiatives in their respective organizations.

The seventeen competencies that were identified as critical for corporate entrepreneurs and entrepreneurial leaders are listed below:

Core Competencies

Corporate Entrepreneur Profile™	
· Accountability	· Motivating
· Adaptability	· Navigating Uncertainty
· Challenge/Growth/Change	· Passionate Communication
· Collaborative	· Problem Solving
· Engaged and Thriving	· Strategic & Analytical Thinking
· Execution	· Takes Action
· Independent Thinking	· Team Builder
· Leadership Effectiveness	· Tolerance for Stress
· Market/Customer Focused	

Each competency consists of a series of five to seven behaviors that, combined make up the competency. There are 33 behaviors in The Devine Inventory® that get allocated to the various competencies. As an example the competency called Leadership Effectiveness is made up of the following behaviors: assertiveness, competitive style, decisiveness, ego, goal-oriented, initiative and time competency. Behaviors are weighted according to their importance to that competency.

The Corporate Entrepreneur Profile™ scores each behavior against a target range for corporate entrepreneurs and the results are rolled up into the appropriate competencies. Each competency is then benchmarked against a database of 10,000 success profiles represented by a percentile score. Any score above 65 percent is considered superior performance. Anything below 38 percent is considered inadequate. Anything in between is considered marginal.

The following diagram shows the average competency scores of the corporate entrepreneurs who participated in our study, ranked high to low. It does not include the competencies of the top scoring corporate entrepreneurs, the entrepreneurial leaders. Both corporate entrepreneurs and entrepreneurial leaders possess the same competencies; entrepreneurial leaders exhibit a greater degree of depth in them. We will look at the competency scores of entrepreneurial leaders in Chapter 5.

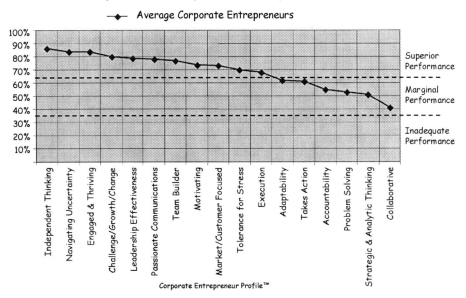

The top six competency scores included the following:

- Independent Thinking

- Navigating Uncertainty

- Engaged and Thriving

- Challenge/Growth/Change

- Leadership Effectiveness

- Passionate Communications

The results show that this was a special group of individuals. The competency scores show that, on average, corporate entrepreneurs are superior in eleven competencies and marginal in six competencies. Corporate entrepreneurs are independent and self-reliant. They deal effectively with ambiguity and are willing to take calculated risks. They are driven and motivated by the excitement of a challenge. They are passionate when they speak about their work and they take pride in making a difference.

It is the subtle differences that set corporate entrepreneurs apart from others. To better understand these subtle differences you will want to take a closer look at the underlying behaviors that make up the corporate entrepreneur competencies. Then compare them to managers and executives in more traditional roles. Although there are a total of 33 behaviors in The Devine Inventory®, we will only look at 18 of them.

The following graph shows some of the key behaviors of corporate entrepreneurs compared to traditional managers and executives. The top line represents the average behaviors of corporate entrepreneurs. The bottom line represents the average behaviors of C-level executives, senior managers, and vice presidents. Behaviors that fall within the six to eight ranges are considered "strengths," three to five "satisfactory," and below three "needs development."

Corporate Entrepreneurs Behaviors

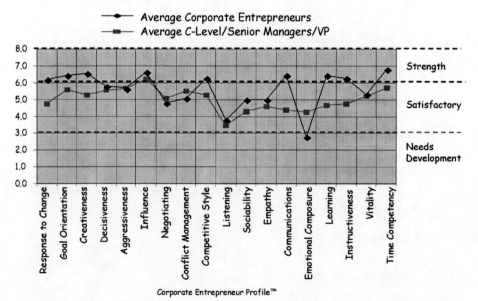

Corporate Entrepreneur Profile™

The results show that on average corporate entrepreneurs score higher than the average for C-level executives, senior managers and vice presidents in a number of key behaviors:

- Response to Change

- Goal Orientation

- Creativeness

- Influence

- Competitive Style

- Communications

- Learning

- Instructiveness

- Time Competency

These results show that corporate entrepreneurs do possess a unique combination of skills and competencies when compared with traditional managers and executives. The results also showed a difference between corporate entrepreneurs and entrepreneurial leaders, and there were gender differences as well. The differences between corporate entrepreneurs and entrepreneurial leaders will be discussed in Chapter 5.

Corporate entrepreneurs scored significantly lower when it comes to emotional composure. They are passionate and wear their emotions on their sleeves. Their feelings are transparent. It doesn't matter if it is in their words or their body language; you know exactly where they stand. They will be open and direct with others. Their passion is for the project, not their own self-interest. Their enthusiasm and passion for the project can be misinterpreted. They often rank low on emotional composure.

Corporate entrepreneurs enjoy working in an environment that is constantly changing because it offers them an opportunity to grow. They are always looking for new opportunities to explore. They are not afraid to move outside their comfort zone. They embrace change.

Corporate entrepreneurs are goal-oriented and believe in setting realistic goals. They are often willing to accept unrealistic or "stretch" goals because they recognize that you have to start with a target, no matter how unrealistic it may be. Spending energy arguing about goals for new investments is often a waste of time. Corporate entrepreneurs know that setting goals can be difficult and that financial targets are estimates at best. Corporate entrepreneurs know what they want to achieve and they will do what it takes to get it done.

Many employees are creative; the difference is coming up with creative ideas that can be implemented and have business value. Corporate entrepreneurs will evaluate an opportunity from all angles and leverage their own experience into the process. They have an ability to look at the idea from concept through to implementation. They are highly creative. They will make decisions quickly and build a case for defending their position. They will integrate intuition and hard data into the evaluation process. They are willing to risk putting their job on the line for their decisions.

Corporate entrepreneurs are aggressive in getting the resources they need to do the job. They recognize that they will not get everything they want, but they use their influencing skills to get as much as they can. They will beg, borrow, and steal resources to make things happen. They are willing to step on toes and break rules to accomplish their task. In turn, they are fair in their negotiations with others and deal effectively in situations where there is conflict. They find a balance between being aggressive and being fair.

Corporate entrepreneurs are competitive when it comes to their project, but less so personally. They recognize the value of being collaborative but know that it takes time to build bridges across organizational boundaries. They are pulled in two directions, feeling compelled to be collaborative but needing to be competitive. Entrepreneurial leaders are better able to balance being competitive and collaborative, as you will see in Chapter 5.

Communications is a critical behavior that most corporate entrepreneurs do well. Corporate entrepreneurs know that they need to be direct and to the point. They are effective in presenting concepts and relaying details. They use relevant examples to generate interest and solicit support. They rank high when it comes to presentation style.

As avid learners, corporate entrepreneurs are always exploring new approaches and solutions to problems. They are eager to learn new things and share their knowledge with others. This enables them to be good at instructing others and helping others develop the skills required to reach objectives. They have an unquenchable need to know, which can at times take them off-track.

Corporate entrepreneurs are very effective in managing their time if it is something of interest to them. They are less effective in completing tasks when doing something that is not as intellectually challenging. Time competency is one of their highest-ranked behaviors.

Over time, corporate entrepreneurs evolve from being independent contributors to good team players. They come to understand the value of teamwork in meeting deadlines and gaining cooperation across organizational boundaries.

Do you have what it takes to be a corporate entrepreneur?

4.2 Meaning of Work

Corporate Entrepreneurs are totally engaged in their work when they are creating and building something. They have an intellectual curiosity to explore new and different approaches to solving problems. They are always looking for novel ways to improve the work environment and customer experience. They are not impressed with titles or structure. They maintain a loose affiliation with the organization and will openly question authority. They have a different perspective on work and easily get bored. *Making a difference is what is important to corporate entrepreneurs.*

A corporate entrepreneur loves charting new territory, exploring the unknown, and experimenting with new ways of working. These are many of the things that the core business is reluctant to tackle, given the risk and uncertainty. Yet these are the very things that the corporate entrepreneur thrives on doing. Corporate entrepreneurs want to create something that will make an impact and have lasting value for the company. For corporate entrepreneurs, making a difference is often more important than climbing the corporate ladder.

Corporate entrepreneurs like to do this type of work because it has meaning for them. They understand the risks involved in tackling new projects. They know the high failure rate of most large projects. They aren't worried about what impact this might have on their career, because they know that climbing the corporate ladder is an old paradigm. They are doing this because they want to learn and grow. They also realize that the value of this work is in the experience itself. They know that win or lose, they will grow from the experience, and then be able to leverage it wherever they go.

Corporate entrepreneurs prefer to work in the beginning stages of a business or product development lifecycle. They may have no interest in moving into the growth phase. Corporate entrepreneurs who develop products are often reluctant to manage those products once they are developed. For them it is more interesting to go back and start a new product.

The following diagram shows where the true corporate entrepreneurs like to work:

Corporate Entrepreneurs
Lifecycle of a Business

If you want to get corporate entrepreneurs totally engaged in their work, give them the toughest challenges. They are energized when the work is challenging and full of ambiguity. Dealing with ambiguity is part of the excitement and challenge they seek. They enjoy the process of sorting through this. There is also a certain level of uncertainty in new ventures. This uncertainty is intellectually challenging and thought-provoking. Finding alternatives and making decisions with limited information is an enjoyable part of the process. Navigating uncertainty is a core competency that many corporate entrepreneurs possess.

You hear a lot about how unhappy many employees are with their current work situation. Surveys suggest that a majority of workers would change jobs if they had the opportunity. It isn't that the work is not interesting—it is often not challenging enough or lacks meaning for the individual. This is especially true with corporate entrepreneurs. They are more likely to walk out the door if they are not challenged.

The more chaotic a situation, the better it is for corporate entrepreneurs. They are not attached to structures and enjoy creating new systems to support their efforts. The more structure you impose, the more frustrated they will become. They prefer the freedom to create new systems and innovative approaches. As a result, they are more loyal to the project than the company. They want the freedom to explore all options.

You may want to consider giving your corporate entrepreneurs the riskier jobs. They are good at taking calculated risks and managing those risks. Part of the excitement of a new venture is the associated risk. They know that the odds are against them, but this is a key motivating factor for corporate entrepreneurs.

Experienced corporate entrepreneurs understand the risks associated with entrepreneurial initiatives. They know going in that there is a high rate of failure. They know there is a possibility that they may decide to leave the company after they have completed the project. Sometimes they feel they have no choice. If the organization cannot offer them a similar opportunity, they will have to weigh the tradeoffs between going back to the core business or taking a position that may have little interest to them.

Corporate entrepreneurs will look for opportunities that will enable them to make a valuable contribution to the corporation. If they don't believe in what they are doing, then they will not give it their best effort. It must be meaningful to them and to the organization for it to be of interest.

The true corporate entrepreneur will seek out opportunities that are fun, exciting, and challenging. In turn, they are not afraid to leave organizations. They are only afraid that they will not find another exciting opportunity.

Are you looking to make a difference or to climb the corporate ladder?

_____

Does your organization provide challenging opportunities?

_____

4.3 Belonging

The concept of developing new communities with common interests is what is driving the growth in blogs. So it is not surprising that corporate entrepreneurs would band together with common interests, skills, desires, and ambitions. They are an extraordinary group of people with a unique combination of skills. Their experience is broad and deep. They understand the highs and lows of building a new business inside a corporation. They are interested in working for something greater than themselves. *Belonging is a human need that resonates with them.*

Belonging to a group of like-minded individuals makes it more rewarding. It isn't just the experience that makes you a corporate entrepreneur, it is also the emotional roller coaster that you go through together. The long nights, the heated debates, and the lack of understanding from the core business enable you to create a bond and common language. These experiences give you an opportunity to see the organization in a new light and it forces you to take a closer look at yourself. All of these factors serve to cement the relationship and synergy between team members.

Being a corporate entrepreneur will require you to face unique obstacles and problems outside of the core business. Whether the new venture is being done in an incubator environment or as part of a corporate venture group, you may have to deal with many organizational and cultural barriers that the rest of the organization doesn't understand. Often you and the team are the only ones who can truly grasp or see these issues. So it is natural for you to console one another and band together to find alternative ways to solve issues. This creates a strong sense of belonging.

As a corporate entrepreneur, you will find yourself evaluating organizational systems that do not support the new business model that you are creating. You will get a new perspective on what needs to change in the core business. As you do, you will slowly unplug from the old systems and create new systems to support your work. This pulls you further away from the core business into a separate and often isolated team environment. It creates anxiety and tension, but it also brings the team members closer together in support of one another.

Eventually, you will feel further and further removed from the core business as the team continues to assert its independence. This is a natural phase in the evolution of the project. You have formed a new culture, operating principles, and ways of dealing with interpersonal dynamics. You've created a new way of working that is foreign to the rest of the organization. They will not understand what you have become. The core business will look very antiquated in comparison.

These are profound times for the team. You will look back at where you have come from and realize that the world of work has changed for you. You look at the core business with a fresh perspective that is unsettling and disturbing. You have become a separate entity with a different set of values and operating practices. It is not clear if you fit into the core business. This realization impacts what you do next.

You belong to a group that has gone through an experience that has changed your perspective on work forever. You know what it means to belong to a group of like-minded individuals and you've experienced what it is to make a difference. Now you and the core business must decide the best way to move forward.

Are you willing to look at the core business in a new light?

Will you be prepared to deal with the consequences of belonging to something different?

4.4 Park Your Ego at the Door

Corporate entrepreneurs are highly intelligent individuals who crave intellectual stimulation. They are interested in promoting their ideas. They have strong sense of self-worth and are confident in their abilities. It is not unusual to find a few individuals who have large egos. They are the prima donnas of the group. They might think that they deserve special treatment, but that is the last thing you want to do. Prima donnas will de-motivate others and create tension on the team. They distract the team's focus and create an adversarial environment. *There is no room for prima donnas on a venture project.*

The thing about high-performance teams is that everyone must be perceived as having an equal stake in the project. That means that each individual must have respect for the other team members. That does not mean that everyone has to like one another, but they do need to respect and acknowledge everyone's contribution.

You will find that many team members don't like one another, but they learn to live with and tolerate each other in pursuit of the end goal.

You quickly learn that the power of the team is far greater than any one individual's contribution. Over time the group dynamics change from one of confrontation to collaboration. You are all in it together. If the project fails, then all of you will have to accept responsibility for the failure. It is the collaborative effort of the team that makes a difference. One individual cannot stand above the rest.

Prima donnas are usually looking out for their own best interests, not those of the team. They are more interested in gaining favor and demonstrating their own professional competency. They want to aggressively promote their own personal agenda. They try to convey to others the very things that don't make them good team players—their intellect, expertise, and individual achievements. They are disruptive and will create unrest in the group. You will be forced to spend time dealing with the emotional turmoil they are likely to create on the team.

To deal with prima donnas, level the playing field. Get the issue off the table early. You can use team-building exercises to expedite this. Team exercises emphasize the need for cooperation between individuals to accomplish tasks. One exercise that is very helpful is pairing people up, blindfolding everyone, and giving them a two-hundred-foot rope and asking them to make a perfect square with it. The rules are that only one pair can make a move at a time. Spending two hours blindfolded while trying to make a perfect square is a great leveler.

In turn, having a healthy ego is good for corporate entrepreneurs. They need to have the confidence to deal with adversity. They need to be tough-minded and stand their ground when they encounter obstacles. They will have to stand up to authority at times and be ready to deal with negativity, resistance, and conflict. Having a healthy ego will help them deal with these. Managing their ego and keeping it in check is what is important.

You can't afford to have prima donnas on your team. They distract others from their work, and as the leader you wind up taking a lot of time managing them. If you find yourself inheriting a team with prima donnas, make a point to deal with them early in the project. It is good to have a team with healthy egos, but keeping them in check will prevent many headaches down the road.

How do you deal with prima donnas on your venture teams?

4.5 Can-Do Attitude

A can-do attitude sets the tone for a venture project and enables individuals to achieve goals beyond their own estimation. Attitudes will change and evolve throughout the project, but keeping a positive attitude will help sustain the momentum and pull you through the tough times. There will always be people out there telling you it can't be done, that you'll never make it. These people don't see what's possible—they only know what isn't. A firm belief in what you are doing and a can-do attitude can take the team a lot further than anyone can imagine. *If you believe you can, you can.*

Corporate entrepreneurs have a mental picture of what is possible. They may not understand the details or exactly how things will get done, but they have a vision firmly planted in their mind. As the project evolves, so does their understanding of what that vision ultimately can become. They gain confidence in their ability to achieve that vision and shape it. They take pride in seeing their vision materialize as they move forward.

A positive attitude gives you hope and serves to reinforce your confidence in what you are doing. It is difficult to sustain a positive attitude all the time when you are creating something that never existed before. You will have doubts and encounter major obstacles along the way. A positive attitude helps you find a way to deal with those doubts and concerns. It strengthens your determination and conviction to find a solution.

When Charles Lindberg said he was going to fly across the Atlantic Ocean, many critics said it couldn't be done. Yet he believed that he could and set out to prove it. He had a positive, can-do attitude that enabled him to believe it was possible. His belief in what he was doing sustained him through the experience.

At times, you will find that your past experiences will slow you down. They cloud your judgment and influence your decision-making. If you knew from your previous experience that something didn't work, you'd say it couldn't be done. Yet someone else believed it could and demonstrated that it could be done. Who would be right? Both of you. One person believed it could be done and did it, another said it couldn't and didn't.

Do not underestimate the power of instilling and maintaining a can-do attitude throughout the venture project. There will be times when doubt creeps in, so deal with it as quickly as possible to turn that attitude around.

How do you instill a can-do attitude into your venture teams?

4.6 Relying on Intuition

An important attribute of being a corporate entrepreneur is being able to rely on intuition. A new venture often faces a number of issues where there isn't always a clear-cut answer. Relying on intuition is often the only way to make a decision. Having a can-do attitude refers to believing that something is possible, but intuition is about going with your gut. It is more of a feeling about something, an internal guidance system that points you in one direction versus another. There are some individuals who possess an uncanny ability to interpret situations by relying on their gut. *Sometimes intuition will have to do.*

Relying on intuition is unnerving for many especially those who are grounded in facts and figures. Management especially may be uncomfortable about these decisions. Any doubts they may have had about the venture going in are often magnified when they hear decisions are being made by relying on someone's gut feeling. Yet it's often these decisions that make the difference and provide another avenue for exploration.

Many corporate entrepreneurs have good influencing skills and are very convincing in their arguments. They can make a solid case for their decision without all the facts and figures, relying much more on intuition. Often it is their belief in what they are doing that enables them to win others over to their point of view.

A decision based on gut is one thing, making a commitment to that decision is another. Corporate entrepreneurs will take the initiative to make unpopular decisions when they feel they are right. They will accurately assess the risk and take the appropriate action when needed. They are not risk takers, they are *calculated* risk takers. Once they make the decision, they commit themselves to it.

Decisions based on intuition should be vetted by testing assumptions about the gut feeling. Often the team's collective wisdom provides enough input to reinforce or dismiss the feeling. Corporate entrepreneurs take responsibility for their decisions, right or wrong. They have confidence in their own abilities to make decisions based on their gut. They are decisive.

A Fortune 100 company decided to invest in a new product line. The company had conducted extensive research to better understand the market need and define the product requirements. They had a solid business plan and were ready to build the team. The entrepreneurial leader, who had not been involved in the initial market research, was concerned about the viability of the business plan.

The leader had a nagging feeling that something was missing and that the product design was not right.

Determined to dismiss their own gut feeling, the team began to dig deeper into the research, went outbound to speak with prospective clients, interviewed internal sales people, and concluded that the product as currently defined would not meet the needs of the target market. By going with their gut feeling, they were able to refine the business plan and readjust expectations to reflect the true reality of the situation. Of course, this increased costs and pushed out delivery dates, but it was better to catch it before the product was further down the development cycle.

Relying on intuition is an under-utilized and underdeveloped skill that organizations must begin to understand. Accepting it will likely be the most difficult part.

Does your organization make decisions based on intuition?

_____

How comfortable are you in making decisions based on intuition?

_____

4.7 Living on the Edge

A corporate entrepreneur will spend a lot of time venturing into uncharted territory. They are the scouts that forge ahead to see what's around the corner or over the mountain. They will encourage and push themselves and their teammates outside of their comfort zones. Some team members will try to hold on to the old way, others will move forward reluctantly, and still others will push ahead with anticipation. Not everyone will be comfortable living on the edge. You may find that it is easier to *let the momentum of the team carry you.*

Living on the edge requires a keen understanding of the perils of choosing the wrong path or making a tactical error that can bring the project to an abrupt halt. Corporate entrepreneurs will need to take risks. They will be called on to make strategic changes in direction and justify their decision with limited data. They will have to retrace their steps to find better alternatives to suit the new direction. They will have to create a new path or a new way and they will be challenged about their decisions.

As a corporate entrepreneur, you will sometimes be forced to choose between two unattractive alternatives. It may force you to maneuver outside the existing policies and procedures of the core business. You will need the courage to take a stand for your convictions. You must be willing to accept the consequences of your decision and acknowledge your mistake if you do not choose wisely.

Being a corporate entrepreneur requires a high tolerance for stress. Individuals must have strong mental, emotional, and physical capacity to sustain the pressure. They must have the mental strength to deal with complexity and ambiguity. They will need to have the emotional composure to deal with organizational resistance, isolation, and uncertainty. They must have the physical energy and vitality to endure long hours and pressure to meet deadlines. Finding the right balance is an individual challenge you will face.

As a corporate entrepreneur you will need to be highly adaptable to changing situations and thrive in an environment of change. You must accept the fact that you will not feel comfortable with all the decisions. There will be times when you will be reluctant to move forward without more data. This resistance will be disruptive. You will find it easier to go with the flow than to put up resistance.

The level of intensity will increase as you move forward. At times you will feel that the team has gone too far, alienated the rest of the organization, broken one too many rules or stood up to authority for the last time. You will come to understand what it means to live on the edge.

How many individuals in your organization are willing to live on the edge?

4.8 Weekend Warriors

Corporate entrepreneurs are adept at managing their own time—they just don't have *enough* time. They recognize that time is a precious commodity for a project and that they must be extremely efficient to meet deadlines. The work and constant distractions can make it difficult to concentrate. They struggle to stay focused and find it difficult to deal with all the details. As a result, corporate entrepreneurs find themselves working long hours and weekends. They know that they can squeeze in more work if they extend the week to weekends. While working on Saturdays should be an option, not a requirement, *the six-day workweek is not unusual.*

Dealing with corporate entrepreneurs is challenging given their high intellect, independence, and creativity. They are always thinking of new ways to approach problems and try new things. This is especially true with "idea people." They find it more difficult to stay focused on a specific task, and are easily bored. They need constant intellectual stimulation to keep them engaged. They can easily distract others and take the team off-track. This wastes time that you cannot afford.

There are others that are strong at bringing things to closure and completing tasks. They will commit to completing tasks and ask for help to meet timetables. They are task-oriented and focused on following through on their commitments. They can work well under pressure. They are your time-savers. They will look for creative ways to accomplish their work on time. Keep them focused on time-sensitive tasks.

The intensity with which teams have to work increases the likelihood that individuals will burn themselves out. They will not always see it coming, so you must stay alert to the signs of burnout. Although they have a high tolerance for stress, they may overestimate their ability to absorb all the stress. Stress can be debilitating and slow things down. Physical exhaustion robs everyone of energy and can cause unnecessary errors that impact time lines.

When you sign up to work on an entrepreneurial project, you soon realize that working long hours is part of the job. The typical workweek for an entrepreneurial team stretches beyond the normal forty-hour week by miles. It isn't unusual for entrepreneurial teams to work through lunches, put in ten—and twelve-hour days, and let work spill over to the weekends. Although it may be necessary to work weekends, it isn't a good practice to encourage it. There will be times when working weekends is unavoidable, but disciplining everyone to work five days per week is healthier.

If you are forced to work weekends, be creative about making it as easy as possible for people. The last thing you want to do is to create more stress. One team allowed parents to bring their children in to visit, and some kept them there all day. The same team invited their spouses to lunch on Saturdays to give them a better handle on what was going on. It let them see firsthand the level of commitment and support that everyone was putting into the project. It put their situation into better perspective.

Despite the long hours, entrepreneurial experiences are exciting and very rewarding. Corporate entrepreneurs work well in stressful environments. They are energized working with others like themselves, but they do not always understand the importance of setting time aside for exercise and fun. Working on Saturdays is not something they like to do, but they are willing to do it. The goal is to improve time competency so that you can minimize working on weekends. In turn, you may want to provide a flexible schedule for corporate entrepreneurs

What are you doing to keep everyone's battery charged?

4.9 Going Home

Entrepreneurial experiences inside existing organizations are revealing. They put everything in a new light. It is a personal and professional experience that will change the way you look at work. The experience forces you take a hard look at yourself and the organization. It changes you, but it may not change the organization. You find yourself living in a different world. You have transitioned to a new way of working. The old rules no longer apply. Going back to the old model is no longer inviting. You begin to wonder if you still fit. *The experience changes your whole perspective on work.*

Unless you have gone through an entrepreneurial experience inside an existing organization, it is difficult to fully understand the experience. You have gone through a change process that you created. You designed, shaped, and tested it along the way. You built a new operating model, culture, and way of working that is now foreign to the rest of the organization. You have left the old model behind and embraced a new model of working. You have enhanced your skills as a corporate entrepreneur. You now know what is possible.

Unfortunately, the rest of the organization has not had the same opportunity. They are still operating in the old model that keeps the core business going. They are comfortable in that role and prefer to stick with a proven business model. They aren't interested in taking on new risks and challenges. They would prefer to work the traditional route to the top. That is fine with you. Somebody needs to keep the core business afloat. You, on the other hand, see a new way to grow the business. You have no desire to climb the corporate ladder the traditional way.

Because of this, you are now perceived as a threat. You have demonstrated that there are alternative ways to grow the business. You know how to change the paradigm and accelerate growth. This will rock the very foundation of the core business. Political factions are likely to step in and squash any efforts to promote this new way of operating, because it will threaten their world. They will perceive that it gives you an unfair advantage.

In turn, you will look around and wonder where you go from here. Chances are, you have just completed one of the more exciting jobs in your career and you are ready to take on even bigger challenges. There may be none where you are. You may be offered a line position as a promotion, but that doesn't seem to excite you. You have reached a point on the road where you must decide if you are going back or moving forward.

A number of corporate entrepreneurs decide to leave their companies after they have completed an entrepreneurial project. Often they feel that they have no choice. During their experience they've grown and stretched themselves beyond what they thought was possible. They recognize that unless the core business can offer them another similar opportunity, they know they will grow bored. They will be taking a step backward if they stay. They realize that the experience itself has changed them and that they will want to continue to work on similar, challenging opportunities if they are to remain. Perhaps they will go off and start their own firm.

You may have heard the phrase "you can't go home again." It means that you will never be able to go back and see home for what it was when you first experienced it. This is the same type of experience for the corporate entrepreneur. Once you've had the experience of being on an entrepreneurial project, you will find it difficult to go back to the core business.

Although there is a lot of talk about the talent shortage and the need for organic growth, there are still very few companies that acknowledge corporate entrepreneurs as a critical corporate resource. Corporate entrepreneurs are the engines of the growth, the change agents. But until organizations begin to understand the value of corporate entrepreneurs and entrepreneurial leaders, these people will probably continue to walk out the door.

Corporate entrepreneurs are the future, and the hope is that more organizations will wake up to this reality and actively recruit them.

Are you willing to change yourself, even if the organization doesn't change?

_____

Are you prepared to deal with the consequences of being a corporate entrepreneur?

_____

SUMMARY: Chapter 4: Pioneers Chart a New Course—
Corporate Entrepreneurs

Corporate entrepreneurs are the pioneers who passionately forge ahead to see what is around the next bend. The small nuances are what set corporate entrepreneurs apart from other employees. They possess a unique combination of behaviors that enable them to work effectively in challenging and high-stress situations. They thrive in an environment of change because they are eager to grow, but are easily bored. They enjoy developing new ideas and approaches to solve problems and exploit untapped opportunities. They find ways to work around organizational obstacles. They maintain a loose affiliation with the organization and are more likely to question authority.

Corporate entrepreneurs don't feel like they fit into traditional organizational roles. They live in a world that is foreign to the rest of the organization. They find themselves striking a balance between being competitive and collaborative, independent and good team players, strategic and tactical. They look at every situation as an opportunity to learn, even if it requires taking risks and making decisions without enough information. They have strong egos and are emotionally involved in what they are doing. They are fair in their negotiations but willing to cut their losses when appropriate.

Innovation projects provide an opportunity for corporate entrepreneurs test their skills and capabilities. They are not focused on climbing the corporate ladder; they are focused on making a difference. Work must have meaning for them if they are to stay actively engaged. They enjoy working with like-minded coworkers who are focused on changing the company for the better. They understand the power of teamwork in getting things done and leveraging the group's collective wisdom. They may not like everyone, but they respect people for what they do and what they contribute to the group.

Corporate entrepreneurs have strong beliefs in what they are doing. They know that anything is possible if they stay focused and stick to their convictions. They may rely on intuition when the answers are not readily available to them. They are always living on the edge, scanning the horizon, trying to determine how to do things differently. They will work until they are exhausted and take little time for themselves. They will come to see themselves and the organization in a new light and it will be difficult for them to step back into the core business. They have seen what is possible and they know what the organization can become if they stay the course.

Corporate entrepreneurs are always looking for new ways to move the company forward.

Corporate Entrepreneur Insights and Lessons Learned

- Energy—"There is a difference between those who love what they are doing and those who do it as a job. Corporate entrepreneurs love what they do."

- Eating the Big Fish—"We love a challenge, the bigger the better."

- Freedom—"Being a corporate entrepreneur gives you a certain range of freedom that is very motivating. You have the freedom and flexibility to try new things that the core business would not think of doing."

- No Safety Net—"There is no safety net when you are working on a project like this. It gives you the confidence to think bigger and take risks."

- Test Skills—"When times are tough, you test your skills."

- Rewards—"Corporate entrepreneurs are not in it for the money. It is the success of the idea that is important."

- Restless Spirits—"Corporate entrepreneurs are restless spirits. They have a high level of energy and need to be doing things that are exciting and challenging. If they aren't, they are restless."

- Passion—"You have to be passionate about what you are doing. It can turn into a cause and take on a life of its own."

- Can-Do Attitude—"In such an endeavor, optimism prevails and a can-do attitude can buy a lot of leverage, but leadership makes the difference."

- Sacrifice—"You forgo a little bit of your personal life to do this. It can take a toll on your family."

- Product Manager versus Corporate Entrepreneur—"There seems to be an evolution from being a product manager to being a corporate entrepreneur."

- Independent Agent—"Eventually I got a reputation as an independent agent. Organizations don't know how to deal with independent people."

- Career—"In most companies there is no career future for CE. Large companies don't want people to be entrepreneurial. They are still operating in a command-and-control environment."

- Corporate Entrepreneurs versus Entrepreneurs—"I had far more resources in large companies. It was easier to develop innovative products inside an organization. After being both (entrepreneur and corporate entrepreneur), I prefer being a corporate entrepreneur."

Chapter 5

Builders Create the Future

Entrepreneurial Leaders

5.1 Hidden Talent—a unique combination of *competencies*

5.2 Business Architects—*design and build* an entrepreneurial mindset and infrastructure

5.3 Conductor—excel at *integrating* limited resources to meet objectives

5.4 A People—A people *hire A people*, B people hire C people

5.5 Breaking Rules—set expectations that you may have to *break rules.*

5. 6 Alone on Island—*isolation* and *resistance* is the loneliest part of the job

5.7 Valley of Despair—each project *hits a wall* that will dramatically change the team

5.8 Willing to be Fired—you must do what's *right* for the project

Corporate Entrepreneur Insights and Lessons Learned

5.1 Hidden Talent

Entrepreneurial leaders are highly effective at leading and building high-performance teams. They thrive in an environment of change and are motivated by the excitement of a challenge. They are independent and loyal at the same time. They prefer the freedom to create new and innovative approaches. They deal proactively with ambiguity and the unknown. Entrepreneurial leaders are highly adaptable, collaborative, and take action when needed. They are good strategic thinkers, excellent problem-solvers, and good at execution. *Entrepreneurial leaders are a hidden talent in most organizations.*

This chapter highlights some of the differences between individuals who are corporate entrepreneurs and those individuals who excel as corporate entrepreneurs, entrepreneurial leaders. The lack of a clear definition of what makes a good corporate entrepreneur makes it even more difficult to define what makes a good entrepreneurial leader. The business literature is quick to throw all leaders into the same bucket. They use attributes and personality styles that align with good leadership practices. Unfortunately, there is little research that makes a distinction between traditional leaders and entrepreneurial leaders.

Experienced entrepreneurial leaders see a difference. They recognize that many of the traditional attributes are fine for business as usual, but do not cut it when it comes to new growth initiatives. These types of initiatives require a set of skills and competencies that many traditional leaders do not possess. The competencies themselves are not so different, it is the *combination* of competencies that makes the difference and the degree to which people possess each competency. Our research has shown this to be true.

The 17 competencies that were identified as critical for corporate entrepreneurs and entrepreneurial leaders are listed below.

Core Competencies

Corporate Entrepreneur Profile™	
· Accountability	· Motivating
· Adaptability	· Navigating Uncertainty
· Challenge/Growth/Change	· Passionate Communication
· Collaborative	· Problem Solving
· Engaged and Thriving	· Strategic & Analytical Thinking
· Execution	· Takes Action
· Independent Thinking	· Team Builder
· Leadership Effectiveness	· Tolerance for Stress
· Market/Customer Focused	

As an entrepreneurial leader, you will need to determine which competencies are most important for your organization. This will enable you to create an internal benchmark to identify, develop, and retain your most entrepreneurial talent. The Corporate Entrepreneur Profile™ provides an initial benchmark to get you started. You can customize it to reflect your organization's unique needs.

Each competency is benchmarked against a data base of 10,000 success profiles. The percentage represents a percentile score. Any score above 65 percent is considered superior performance. Anything below 38 percent is considered inadequate. Anything in between is considered marginal.

The following diagram shows the competencies of entrepreneurial leaders, ranked from high to low.

Entrepreneurial Leader Competencies

— ◆ — Average Entrepreneurial Leaders

100%	
90%	Superior
80%	Performance
70%	
60%	Marginal
50%	Performance
40%	
30%	Inadequate
20%	Performance
10%	

Competencies (x-axis, left to right): Independent Thinking, Navigating Uncertainty, Engaged & Thriving, Challenge/Growth/Change, Leadership Effectiveness, Tolerance for Stress, Execution, Problem Solving, Market/Customer Focused, Adaptability, Passionate Communication, Accountability, Motivating, Team Builder, Takes Action, Collaborative, Strategic & Analytic Thinking

Corporate Entrepreneur Profile™

The results show that this was an extraordinary group of individuals. The competency scores show that, on average, entrepreneurial leaders are superior in all 17 competencies.

The top six competency scores included the following:

• Independent Thinking

• Navigating Uncertainty

- Engaged & Thriving

- Challenge/Growth/Change

- Leadership Effectiveness

- Tolerance for Stress

Entrepreneurial leaders have a depth and breadth of experience that set them apart from their peers. They excel across a wide spectrum of competencies. They enjoy exploring new territory and dealing with uncertainty. They are willing to question and challenge current thinking. They are energized when presented with a problem or opportunity. They are effective in managing limited resources and leveraging resources across organizational boundaries. They have a higher tolerance for stress that enables to operate effectively under extreme pressure and stress.

The following diagram shows the differences between corporate entrepreneurs and entrepreneurial leaders. The top line shows the competency scores for the entrepreneurial leaders. The bottom line shows the corresponding competencies for the corporate entrepreneurs.

Entrepreneurial Leaders versus Corporate Entrepreneurs

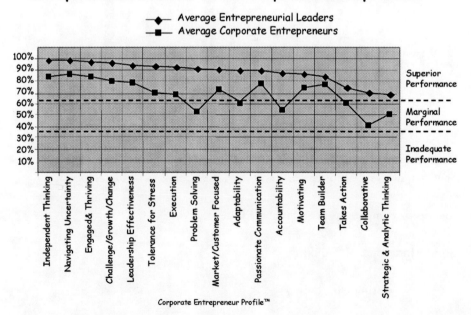

Corporate Entrepreneur Profile™

Entrepreneurial leaders scored higher than the corporate entrepreneurs in all 17 competencies and significantly higher in six of the competencies: accountability, adaptability, collaborative, execution, problem-solving, and tolerance for stress. These are some of the competencies that set them apart from corporate entrepreneurs. Entrepreneurial leaders in particular exhibit a wide range of skills and competencies that enable them to excel in entrepreneurial settings.

Although this is useful data for identifying and selecting entrepreneurial individuals, it does not tell us what competencies are the most critical. To determine which competencies were most important, the corporate entrepreneurs and entrepreneurial leaders who participated in our research were asked to prioritize the competencies in terms of their importance to the successful execution of their job.

The top seven competencies the corporate entrepreneurs and entrepreneurial leaders identified as being a priority were: accountability, challenge/growth/change, collaborative, execution, problem solver, takes action and team builder.

Top Priority Competencies

Priorities	Corporate Entrepreneurs	Entrepreneurial Leaders
Accountability	Marginal	Superior
Challenge/Growth/Change	Superior	Superior
Collaborative	Marginal	Superior
Execution	Superior	Superior
Problem Solving	Marginal	Superior
Takes Action	Marginal	Superior
Team Builder	Superior	Superior

The results showed that, on average, corporate entrepreneurs scored high in three of the priority competencies and the entrepreneurial leaders performed high in all of them.

Identifying, developing, and retaining entrepreneurial talent will be one of your greatest challenges. Entrepreneurial leaders are always looking for a new challenge. They get bored easily and are willing to leave to find the next opportunity.

What is your organization doing to identify and develop entrepreneurial leaders?

___

What is your organization doing to retain this critical corporate resource?

___

5.2 Business Architects

Entrepreneurial leaders design and build new growth businesses. These leaders are less likely to have a political agenda. They have an organizational agenda that speaks to the need for the organization to move to a new operating model. They know that the old model gets in the way and they are willing to take unpopular positions. They understand the need for change and they are eager to lead that change. Tearing down old systems and rebuilding new ones is part of the job. *They are business architects who design and build the entrepreneurial mindset and infrastructure for growth.*

These leaders assert a certain amount of independence, but are also loyal to the core business. Their loyalty is divided between the organization and their project. They need a certain degree of independence and autonomy to break through barriers and set up new systems. Over time, their loyalties will shift to the project as new systems are created to support a more entrepreneurial environment. They are often forced to make tough decisions that will test their loyalty to the company. It will come down to doing what is right, versus what is politically correct.

Entrepreneurial leaders understand the strategic significance of their project to the company's overall goals. They can envision the financial, political, and cultural impact these changes will have on the organization. They know the boundaries of the organization and recognize where they are flexible and where they are not. The project will test the limits of those boundaries. It will be necessary to push those boundaries beyond what is currently thought possible—and accept responsibility for the results.

Entrepreneurial leaders set the tone for the entire project by establishing an operating framework to support their efforts. They create organizational structures that are fluid and changeable. They create new systems and processes to support the end goals. They set new standards for productivity and performance. They reward risk-taking and initiative. They build a new entrepreneurial culture.

As the entrepreneurial leader, you will be designing and building a new infrastructure to support corporate entrepreneurship as you move forward. It is something that evolves over time. The goal will be to leverage the existing systems, policies, and practices of the core business, but that is often easier said than done. You will need to determine which systems, policies, and practices work and which ones don't. There is no research that describes the best type of operating environment for corporate entrepreneurship.

The Corporate Entrepreneurial Infrastructure™ workshop was designed to help entrepreneurial leaders build the entrepreneurial mindset and infrastructure they need to develop entrepreneurship as a core competency in their organization.

Entrepreneurial Mindset and Infrastructure

Corporate Entrepreneurial Infrastructure™			
Create Entrepreneurial Mindset	Define Operating Framework	Develop the Roadmap	Final Presentation
Opportunities/ Problems	Alternatives	Validation	Solution

The goal of the workshop is to transform the way your organization works and more effectively grow your business. The workshop ensures that the right people and processes are in place to accelerate business growth, minimize risks, and increase success rates. This action learning workshop was designed to enable you to take the lead in helping your organization build the following capabilities.

- Develop the leadership skills needed to operate differently

- Create cross functional collaboration to support new ideas

- Instill program management discipline into operating practices

- Define the operating framework required for success

- Provide the tools, techniques and practices needed to be more effective

- Build execution competencies to increase buy-in and execution

As an entrepreneurial leader these are the things that you will need to do to build the entrepreneurial mindset and infrastructure in your organization. The workshop provides the basic fundamentals, the team integrates them into their work practices. This ensures that what is learned in the workshop is applied and reinforced throughout the process.

Entrepreneurial leaders are business architects that design, build and execute. They are true entrepreneurs in that sense. Although entrepreneurial leaders exhibit a high degree of independence, they are still very loyal employees. They are more entrepreneurial in their behavior. Their affiliation is more aligned with the project than the company. They are committed to their own personal values and those of the team, but they recognize that what they are doing is for the core business.

Entrepreneurial leaders create the mindset and develop the entrepreneurial infrastructure for success. They create the change that is required to transform the organization.

How do you create the entrepreneurial mindset and infrastructure for success?

5.3 Conductor

Entrepreneurial leaders combine their strategic and analytic thinking with their ability to effectively plan activities and manage resources. They have an ability to think strategically and tactically while integrating a healthy dose of reality into the equation. They see how their project fits into the bigger picture and understand the implications if they are not successful. They also realize that they will not have all the resources they need to get the job done, so they build bridges across organizational boundaries. They find creative ways to leverage the skills they have. *Entrepreneurial leaders excel at integrating limited resources to meet objectives.*

As the conductor, you are not expected to be an expert on everything, but you must make sure that each individual is performing at their highest potential. It also means that each individual must continue to work at the same or similar pace as everyone else. If one person is not keeping pace, the rest of the team may suffer. Ensuring that everyone is on the same page, playing the same tune, at the same pace will be one of the more rewarding things you do.

An entrepreneurial leader develops a high-performance team as quickly as possible. It is normal to inherit many good individual contributors who are not necessarily good team players. Often these individuals have been successful because they have excelled as individuals. Now they are being asked to be part of a team. They will be required to develop a new way of working. They will encounter obstacles they have never dealt with before. They will be looking to you, the leader, to set the stage.

Chances are you will have limited or no control over other resources. You will be forced to find creative ways to gain support and solicit their cooperation. You may even try to co-opt some of them to join the team. Managing resources out of your control will require finesse and influencing skills. Gaining cooperation will be challenging and extremely frustrating. You are the conductor; getting everyone to work together like a symphony orchestra will be one of your biggest challenges and greatest achievements.

Entrepreneurial leaders will foster collaboration across organizational boundaries to acquire and secure limited resources. They will walk away when they know they are wasting their time and find alternative ways to accomplish specific tasks. Being competitive is a core competency and so is being collaborative. You will have to find the right balance between the two.

Entrepreneurial leaders have the ambition and the skills to achieve challenging goals. They are confident in their ability to deal with obstacles and organizational roadblocks. They use team-building to motivate and drive others to task completion. They use their creativity to find innovative solutions to pressing problems. Execution is a core competency of entrepreneurial leaders.

Over time, entrepreneurial leaders will find they are doing less and less. It is just like the orchestra conductor who does the directing, while the musicians accomplish the real work. Then you know that everyone is playing like a symphony orchestra.

Can you create a high-performance team that operates like a symphony orchestra?

5.4 A People

Entrepreneurial leaders thrive in a learning environment, so it is not surprising that they would see a new venture initiative as a great new learning opportunity. They enjoy learning new things, are highly intelligent, and self-confident. They have a healthy ego and are competent in their ability to get things done. They value having highly skilled and intelligent individuals like themselves on a team. For these reasons, they are more likely to attract and hire A people to their project. *A people hire A people, B people hire C people.*

A people are strong, confident, self-motivated, decisive, and highly productive individuals. They realize that in order to grow, they must step outside of their comfort zone. They love a challenge, are highly competitive and less likely to feel threatened by other A people. B people, on the other hand, are often less sure of themselves, slower to adapt, less willing to take risks, and unlikely to hire someone smarter, brighter or more confident than themselves. As a result, they are more likely to select C people, who are less capable, in order to maintain a certain degree of control.

Good entrepreneurial leaders will select A people for their team. It may be more challenging for them, but they know that the positives outweigh the negatives. It stands to reason that a good entrepreneurial leader would be an A person. An A person is more likely to feel comfortable leading a team of A people, because he or she is comfortable delegating responsibility and ownership to the team. An A person recognizes that in order to keep the team motivated and engaged, the leader will need to stretch people and coach them when they step way beyond the boundaries of their own comfort zones.

Entrepreneurial leaders are more inclined to delegate responsibility to the team. They know that giving the team the authority to speak on their behalf gives them the confidence they will need to grow quickly. Corporate entrepreneurs are eager to take on new responsibilities and test their abilities. They are confident in their ability to find new and creative ways to get things done. They look at every situation as an opportunity to grow. Not all entrepreneurial leaders are extroverts; some are introverts who may prefer to delegate and are comfortable having team members take the lead.

An entrepreneurial leader will have to be tolerant and allow people to make mistakes and learn from them. A leader must know when to step in and turn things around and when to let the team solve the problem on their own. They will have to deal with the emotional and behavioral roller coaster that each individual will encounter along the way. Corporate entrepreneurs are passionate about what they do and openly express their emotions verbally or through body language.

Not everyone on a team can be an A player, nor will they perform at the same level of productivity. It will be important to align individuals who complement each others strengths and weaknesses. The leader must understand the skills, behaviors, and aptitudes of each individual under normal and stressful times. They know that it can be useful for them and the team to understand the different styles and how to work more effectively. Teams that understand the underlying personality and behaviors are more likely to respect those differences and leverage them. It also helps identifying the A, B, and C players on a team.

Team members who are A players are often extremely challenging to work with. They are highly productive and highly disruptive at the same time. But they are the people you will want on your team.

Do you select A people to be your entrepreneurial leaders?

Are you selecting A, B, or C people for your entrepreneurial teams?

5.5 Breaking Rules

Part of being an entrepreneurial leader is charting a new course—and that means breaking down barriers that get in your way. Leaders are open to negotiating and dealing with conflict, but they also know when to cut their losses and move on. At some point they may be forced to step on toes, tick people off, and break rules to get things done. Establishing this up front with the CEO and sponsor will be useful. Letting them know in advance will make it easier to discuss when it actually happens. Inevitably, you will wind up reminding them of that conversation down the road. *Set expectations that you may have to break some rules.*

A good practice is establishing a formal contract between the entrepreneurial leader and the sponsor. Often the role of the sponsor is not clear. Creating a contract formalizes the relationship and serves as the foundation document for ongoing dialogue and communication. The contract forms the basis for the working relationships, establishes the roles and responsibilities, and sets expectations for both parties. You want to be sure that there is no room for interpretation. It makes it clear what is acceptable and what is not. You were hired to lead, so the organization must be open to letting you make the tough calls.

Sponsor Contract

Sponsor Contract

Project Title: _____ Date: _____
Sponsors:_____ Champion:_____
Team Members:
_____
_____

Problem to be solved (3 lines maximum)
_____
_____
_____

Key Deliverables:
1.
2.
3.
4.
5.
6.

Needs from the Sponsor:
Essential: _____ Desirable: _____
_____ _____

Measurements:
1.
2.
3.

Signatures (Team members) _____ (Champion) _____
                                    (Sponsor) _____
_____

Aspects of a Good Contract
Clear Deliverables - Clarity on the problem and knowledge that these deliverables will solve the problem
Measurements – The customer and team will measure success in the same way
Standards – The customer and team agree on what is passing and what is outstanding
Reward is tied to Standard – Clarity on what the reward will be for passing and for excellence
Clear Assessment Process – Clarity on who will assess the progress of contract and when
Mid Course Correction Built In – We don't know what we don't know so dates have been identified to review the project and correct the direction

Orchard Consulting

Entrepreneurial leaders prefer to have minimal supervision and are not afraid to question authority or challenge the status quo. They support the organization's goals; they just prefer to be more independent. They respect authority, but do things their way. They are willing to try new things regardless of the consequences and are willing to challenge the rules that do not serve the project's best interests. They may do the same with peers and across organizational boundaries. They do what it takes to move the project forward.

There will be plenty of times when unexpected issues arise that require immediate attention. Entrepreneurial leaders must be decisive and make judgment calls that are counter to existing organizational practices. These leaders are willing to be held accountable and will accept responsibility for their actions. The sponsor must be willing to support them, even if they wouldn't sanction their actions.

Entrepreneurial leaders have a high respect for the organization and will not take unnecessary risks. They understand that in order for them to be successful, the organization must change. They are willing to push the limits of what is possible and break down barriers that get in their way.

How tolerant is your organization when individuals break rules?

5.6 Alone on An Island

Can you imagine being stranded on a desert island with hundreds of boats sailing by and nobody seeming to notice you? Well, if you have ever been an entrepreneurial leader, you know what it's like dealing with isolation. It is the loneliest part of the job. It isn't as if you are alone in the organization, it's that you find yourself sailing alone, often against the tide. You are trying to do new things, you are charting a new course, and you are making waves. *Dealing with isolation and resistance is one of the loneliest parts of the job.*

Not everyone understands or accepts what you are doing. It's as if you are sitting on the other side of the continent. You are the one charting a new course, laying a new foundation, experimenting, creating new methods and processes. You are creating a new world. Yet you know you must co-exist with the core business, so you balance the tradeoffs of what policies, procedures, systems, and measures fit and which don't. You have no guide to show you the way. You are often on your own.

Part of the isolation comes from not having a resource who fully understands what you are experiencing. Unless someone has been an entrepreneurial leader, they can only imagine what it is like. Since you are often blazing a new path, you are the one who sees the situation most clearly, and it will often be difficult for others to see things the same way. You may be able to bounce ideas around with others, but the clarity with which you see it can only be shared by someone else who's experienced it.

Another part of the isolation is the resentment and resistance you get from your peers and others in the organization. New initiatives are in the spotlight, with much attention and focus given to promoting the new and maintaining the old. There will always be a faction in the existing organization that is hoping you will fail. It is easier for them to sit on the sidelines and watch until they get a better handle on whether you will succeed or fail. It often comes down to a fear of change. If the project succeeds, then things will change and they will need to change.

The resistance you face can slow things down. Understanding why you are getting resistance can help you deal with it more effectively. People resist for a number of reasons including a loss of control, uncertainty, surprises, past resentment, perceived or real threats and fears. This resistance is often expressed in their words and actions. "Give me more details" or "this is impractical" or "I'm not surprised, we have tried this before." Keep in mind that the resistance is rational to the resistor but may not seem logical to you as the observer. Dealing with resistance when you encounter it may be easier then letting the situation go unresolved.

In many cases you are transitioning to a new organizational model that is uncertain. Many people will be reluctant to accept the new model until it has proven itself. There is a certain level of risk in embracing the new. This is especially true if the organization is experimenting with many new business opportunities. One entrepreneurial leader talked about the fact that their organization started so many new initiatives and finished so few that the organization viewed every new initiative as the "initiative of the quarter." The rest of the organization was not willing to support or embrace any new ones until they were solidly entrenched in the organization.

Isolation and resistance is the toughest part of the job. It is discouraging and it makes life tougher for the leader and the team.

How are you helping your entrepreneurial leaders deal with isolation?

5.7 Valley of Despair

Every entrepreneurial initiative eventually hits a wall called the "valley of despair." This is a point when the project gets bogged down, people are totally stressed, a negative attitude permeates the team, and progress slows to a crawl. Team members will get discouraged, spend time complaining, give up, and some will even quit. When you get to this point you will know it. Understanding what it is, planning for it, and dealing with it appropriately will get you through, but it isn't easy, it isn't always fast, and it will take all the energy and emotion that you have left as a leader to manage through it. *Each project will hit a wall that will dramatically change the team.*

The challenge is recognizing that most projects reach a point where they face their own "valley of despair." Preparing the team for this and helping them through it will be challenging. They need to understand that it is a normal part of the process. They are transitioning to a new operating model and leaving the old model behind. There is anxiety in moving from something that is grounded and secure to something more fragile. Each person will react differently, but if they anticipate it they can deal more effectively with it.

In turn, it's important that you prepare your sponsor and the CEO for this event. It will not only enable them to assist you through this process, but it also provides you with a sounding board. Like you, they must realize that the pressure and stress have been building to a point where the team can't take much more. The team will be tired, short-tempered, and rude to one another. They will find fault with things that they totally accepted before. The stress and pressure are natural byproducts of such an effort.

The valley of despair is not an event but a process that builds up. A team will naturally be energetic and enthusiastic at the beginning. Once they get deeply entrenched in the project, they often lose sight of why they are doing it in the first place. They ask themselves if the stress and pressure are worth it. They begin to question the viability of what they are doing. Fear begins to run rampant throughout the team that they will not make it. Like dominoes, one person's fears play on another's until everyone is involved. The team slides further and deeper into the valley of despair.

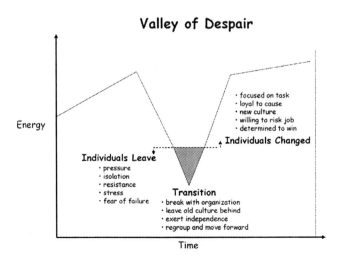

Valley of Despair

At this point some people decide they've had enough and ask to go back into the core business. Others will decide it is time to leave. Either way, it has an impact on the team and organization. As the entrepreneurial leader, you will be trying to hold things together and find alternative solutions to fill the gaps. You begin to go through the same process as the team. You will need the support and encouragement of the CEO and sponsor to keep you energized. You may start having your own doubts.

As the team slides into the valley of despair, they will reach a transition point. This is when the team needs you the most. It is physically and emotionally draining. The team needs to stop and catch their breath. Pushing harder will only make things worse. They need to regroup and recalibrate where they are. They must put new plans in place to pick up the slack, find alternative resources to fill the gaps. This can be reenergizing and start to build back some of the confidence they have lost.

The team will then begin to build back momentum, turn the corner, and climb out of the valley of the despair. They have made the transition and have broken away from the core business. They are still scared and a little shaky, but they get back on track. These individuals will be changed forever because they made it through and reached the other side. They have created a new way of working and they have left the old systems behind. They can look back and see the core business for what it is and what they know it can become.

You may never really understand what triggered the slide toward the valley of despair. It could be organizational pressure, time pressure, or self-imposed pressure. In most cases the team realizes that much is riding on the project and there is a growing feeling that they may not make it. It is as if you are stuck in quicksand or moving in slow motion.

Going through the valley of despair is part of the process. It will test the patience and resolve of the entrepreneurial leader.

Have you ever experienced the "valley of despair"?

5.8 Willing to Be Fired

As the entrepreneurial leader, you've made a commitment to the team and the project. Your loyalty will slowly shift from the corporation to the project. You are not abandoning the corporation; you have recognized that you cannot develop the project under the existing rules and procedures of the organization. Therefore, you will at times be forced to make decisions that may put your job on the line. *You must come in every day and be willing to be fired for what you believe is the right thing to do for the project.*

There are ten criteria you can use to determine if you have what it takes to be a corporate entrepreneur and one of them is willing to be fired.

The Intrapreneurs Ten Commandments

1. Build your team, intrapreneuring is not a solo activity.
2. Share credit wisely.
3. Ask for advice before you ask for resources.
4. Under promise and over deliver – publicity triggers the corporate immune system.
5. Do any job needed to make your dream work, regardless of your job description.
6. Remember it is easier to ask for forgiveness than for permission.
7. Keep the best interests of the company and its customers in mind, especially when you have to bend the rules or circumvent the bureaucracy.
8. Come to work each day willing to be fired.
9. Be true to your goals, but be realistic about how to achieve them.
10. Honor and educate your sponsor.

Pinchot & Company

This willingness to put your job on the line is an attribute and characteristic that is prevalent among corporate entrepreneurs. A corporate entrepreneur is focused on moving the organization forward. They realize that if things are going to change, they will have to do things differently. They may be the only person in a meeting without a personal agenda. Their agenda is to get the project completed so they will do whatever it takes to accomplish that task.

You must walk in every day and do what's right for the project. That includes making decisions that are unpopular or don't support the party line. If you were an external entrepreneur, you would have to make the same tough decisions to move your business forward.

Once the entrepreneurial leader and team have shifted their loyalty from the organization to the team, it will be difficult to stop the momentum and conviction that everyone brings to the project. There is a renewed sense of determination and drive to move the project forward at all cost. Teams will work around the clock to meet deadlines or sacrifice time with their family to complete their work. This behavior is exactly what you can expect to see, and it is often a sign that the team has emerged from the valley of despair.

The willingness to put your job on the line for what you believe is part of the makeup required for good entrepreneurial leaders. It demonstrates that they are willing to make the tough decisions despite the consequences.

Are your entrepreneurial leaders willing to be fired?

SUMMARY: Chapter 5: Builders Create the Future— *Entrepreneurial Leaders*

Entrepreneurial leaders find a clear distinction between themselves and traditional leaders. They understand the breadth and depth of experience that is required to lead an entrepreneurial initiative. It isn't that they have different competencies; it is that they have a unique combination of competencies and behaviors. The top six competencies for entrepreneurial leaders include independent thinking, navigating uncertainty, engaged and thriving, challenge/growth/change, leadership effectiveness, and passionate communicators. Entrepreneurial leaders exhibited higher scores than traditional leaders in a majority of the 33 behaviors in the Corporate Entrepreneur Profile™. There are gender differences and distinctions between entrepreneurial leaders and corporate entrepreneurs.

These individuals are the hidden talent in many organizations. On the surface, they appear to exhibit some of the same characteristics as traditional leaders. Yet they understand that developing new initiatives inside existing organizations is a balancing act. They must live in two different worlds: the new world they are creating and the core business. They are the business architects who are building an infrastructure to support the new growth business. They build the entrepreneurial mindset and infrastructure along the way. They are creating a new culture as they go.

Entrepreneurial leaders run up against an entrenched culture and systems, processes, and procedures that do not support their efforts. They will be asked to lead a group of people who may have never dealt with the stress and complexity of building a new business inside an existing one. They are more likely to hire A people who are strong, self-confident, self-motivated, and decisive to be on the team. They know that having a mix of internal and external employees will provide new insights and challenge traditional thinking. They know that they must turn these individuals into a highly productive team as quickly as possible.

Entrepreneurial leaders know that they will run up against roadblocks. They are prepared to break rules, step on toes, and make unpopular decisions. They know that things will have to change to move forward. They prefer minimal supervision and the freedom to question authority. They are loyal to the corporation, but they are more loyal to the project. At times they will feel like they are all alone on an island. They will encounter resistance and pressure from their peers and others in the organization. They will have to deal with the emotional roller coaster and keep things together when the team hits the wall known as the "valley of despair." They are willing to put their job on the line for the project.

Entrepreneurial leaders are the business builders who turn ideas into businesses.

Corporate Entrepreneur Insights and Lessons Learned

- Power—"Power doesn't drive me. The excitement of the challenge does."

- Flourish—"You flourish in an environment where you are not constrained by existing rules."

- Performance—"I had the hardest job because it was difficult to know how I was doing. We had to create new ways to measure progress."

- Tea Leaves—"You need to constantly read the tea leaves so you can be proactive, rather than react to situations once they occur. There can be big ramifications for the project."

- Pulling Back—"You need to pull back once in a while and look at the project from the organization's perspective. You can lose sight of the importance of the project, given changing priorities."

- Resentment. "We were getting all the attention, funding and resources. We were the rising stars. I think we were a threat to the rest of the organization. They were not very supportive, so we had to find ways to do it on our own."

- Personal Agenda—"I remember sitting in an executive review meeting and when it was over, someone turned to me and said, 'You are the only one in the room without a personal agenda.' Everyone else was there promoting, preserving and pushing their own personal and professional agenda. I was building a business."

- Permission—"I chose not to see the corporate walls and silos. That gave me the permission to explore the best way to build the business."

- Breaking Rules—"I needed to prove a point so I broke one of the rules. My boss read me the riot act, slapped me on the wrist, and asked me to atone for my sins. I knew she agreed with my decision, but had to reprimand me anyway."

- Failure—"If you had a prior track record of success, you were allowed a margin of error. Otherwise there was no room for failure. Failure was not tolerated."

- Bet Your Job—"In our organization you had to be willing to bet your job when you signed up to lead a new initiative, because failure was not an option. Even if you did a bang-up job, you usually only got a pat on the back. Risk and reward were out of balance."

- Peak Experience—"This project was the high point of my experience. I felt so passionate and excited about the work. It was the best time of my career."

Chapter 6

Engage Teams So They Thrive

Team Dynamics

6.1 Hold on to Your Hats—set *expectations* that it will be a bumpy ride

6.2 Me, You and Us—have clear *roles and responsibilities*

6.3 Soul of Project—*team values* and passion are at the core of every project

6.4 Stretching People—taking people outside their comfort zone helps them *grow*

6.5 Two Days in Woods—nature is a forum for building a *high-performance* team

6.6 Lead by Following—delegating *control* to the team keeps things moving

6.7 Tell Us What to Do—the team may defer to the leader to make *decisions* faster

6.8 Getting Unstuck—dealing with *conflict and tension* is critical to getting unstuck

6.9 Struggle for Legitimacy—swimming upstream against the *culture*

Corporate Entrepreneur Insights and Lessons Learned

6.1 Hold on to Your Hat

Being part of a corporate entrepreneurial initiative is a lot like riding a roller coaster. At times it can be exhilarating and at others it can plunge you to the depths of despair. True corporate entrepreneurs love the highs, the lows, the long hours, the heated debates, and the pressure to deliver something new. They are motivated by the excitement of being part of the future and making a difference. If you decide to come along for the ride, you must be prepared to hold on to your hat, because it will be a bumpy ride. *Set expectations that it will be a bumpy ride.*

Individuals who are eager to join an entrepreneurial initiative may not understand the demands that such an endeavor can place on them personally or professionally. It is incumbent upon you to set the proper expectations up front. Given the high failure rate, there is a high probability that the initiative may not be successful. Are prospective team members prepared to deal with the consequences of failure? Are they committed to putting in long nights and weekends? Do they have the tolerance for stress that will be required to deal with the uncertainty? Are they willing to break rules and step on toes to get things accomplished? These are only a few of the things they will need to deal with.

Despite all the rhetoric about the need to have a tolerance for failure, many companies are still unwilling to acknowledge failure as part of the learning process. Those who join an entrepreneurial initiative must be willing to accept the consequences of failure. Depending on how your organization deals with failure, it can be career-limiting or career-enhancing. In most cases, it is not looked upon favorably.

The initial excitement of a new project quickly turns into the harsh reality of aggressive time lines, resource shortages, and limited funding. The team doesn't always factor in the unexpected or think about backup strategies, which create anxiety when things go wrong. They neglect to think about their own ability to absorb the stress or take into account the toll that long hours might have on their health or family life. They try to work through lunch to pick up precious time when a ten-minute break or a breath of fresh air may be more effective.

Although the pressure to perform is often self-imposed, there comes a time in every project when the pressure seems unbearable. The team starts to get trapped in a negative cycle, things slow down, and progress stalls. Individuals make sacrifices that may jeopardize their personal well-being. Tradeoffs will have to be made between family and work. Some team members will self-select out of a project if the pressure becomes too great. Others will call it quits and leave the company. It is important to find ways to deal with individual and team stress.

Being entrepreneurial requires a certain degree of independence that often pits the individual against the organization. They are loyal to the organization but grow increasingly more loyal to the team and project. They find themselves torn between support for authority and taking measures into their own hands. The tug and pull is uncomfortable. They will be forced to make choices that are unpopular and politically incorrect. These decisions can be gut-wrenching and threatening. You will want to find individuals who are not afraid to ask the tough questions and are willing to try new approaches.

Although corporate entrepreneurs are willing to challenge and question authority they still maintain a healthy respect for authority. You will need to allow people to challenge current thinking. Team players must be able to depend on each other to take responsibility for their own tasks. They will have to rely on others that they have no control over. Politically the team is operating inside the core business. They must learn to live with the values of the core business along with their own values. The team will build its own identity which will separate them from the rest of the organization. This creates tension between the team and the rest of the organization. Team members must realize that they are still a part of a larger organization.

Like an entrepreneurial start-up, you will also be operating in a less formal way. The informal nature of start-ups is foreign to many people with experience in hierarchical organizations. Everyone will be asked to sign up to do things outside of their current responsibilities. You will want to be sure that everyone is comfortable operating in a less structured environment.

Stress is a normal part of work but is magnified many times over when it comes to working on these entrepreneurial projects. It is an inevitable part of the process and it separates those who have the physical and mental capacity to deal with large amounts of stress from those who don't. It can help to find and identify, at the beginning, those individuals with a high tolerance for stress. Individuals with a high tolerance for stress are able to deal with duress in a balanced manner.

At the same time, corporate entrepreneurship is exhilarating and a lot of fun. It is hard work that is extremely rewarding. There is a sense of pride and ownership. There is also the excitement of building something of value and making a contribution. It is a time of discovery and exploration. It is an adventure that you will treasure and look back on with pride.

If you like riding a roller coaster, then you know that it can be a bumpy ride. You will need to be able to deal with both the highs and the lows.

Is your organization able to deal with the ups and downs of entrepreneurial projects?

_____

How does your organization help teams deal with stress?

_____

6.2 Me, You and Us

The goal of any new initiative is to make the team productive as quickly as possible. Building a high-performance team is often dependent on having clear roles and responsibilities. Defining roles and responsibilities up front ensures that everyone has a clear understanding of the big picture and where they fit. This includes the CEO, sponsor, entrepreneurial leader, and team. Roles and responsibilities should also be defined between teams. This helps clarify dependencies and interdependencies, which helps facilitate handoffs and the coordination of activities between groups. It is important to know the difference between me, you and us. *Have clear roles and responsibilities.*

At the executive level, the CEO and sponsor roles should also be clarified up front. CEO endorsement and support sets the tone for the importance of the project to the organization. Entrepreneurial initiatives driven by the CEO are far more likely to succeed than those at lower levels. It is not always possible to get direct CEO involvement, but it is sure nice to have CEO support. You may need the political clout that only the CEO can provide.

In some organizations there is a formal contracting process between the team and sponsor as was discussed in Chapter 5. This ensures that the sponsor and team have identified their respective roles. Sponsors play a critical part in helping smooth the way through organizational obstacles that can be a drain on project resources. In one organization, the sponsor turned over control of the new initiative when he thought it might not succeed, just to protect his political position in the organization. Contracting may not prevent this from happening, but it certainly helps in transferring responsibilities when ownership changes hands.

Clarifying roles and responsibilities across organizational boundaries is also a very useful exercise. Understanding interdependencies will be important in managing resources. Organizations already burdened with their own work are often very reluctant to relinquish precious resources to what may be perceived as another experiment. Establishing roles early in the project signals that cross organizational cooperation and participation is expected.

Establishing roles and responsibilities between the leader and the team is fairly straightforward. Defining roles and responsibilities between different teams may not be. This is why it is critical to ensure that each team understands the interdependencies with the other teams. Establishing roles and responsibilities serve as a launching pad for further clarifying what needs to get done and then assigning specific tasks to various teams. Although roles and responsibilities will change and change often, establishing them up front makes it easier to get started. Keep it simple.

Roles and Responsibilities Matrix

Person	Role	Responsibilities	Team/ Group	Deliverables	Date

Establishing roles up front provides some structure to a rather chaotic process.

What role does the CEO have in your initiative?

_____

Is there a formal contracting process with sponsors?

_____

Are the roles and responsibilities of your team clearly defined?

_____

6.3 Soul of Project

Values are the glue that inspire and hold the team together during good times and bad times. Team values define the moral character of the group. The mechanics of setting up a project can be learned, but team values must be lived. Defining some simple team values at the beginning of a project helps ensure that the team understands what is important to each individual and the collective values of the group. Team values are the soul of any project. They become the guiding principles by which the team interacts with one another and the organization. *Team values and passion are at the core of any project.*

The values the team develops will form the basis for the new culture. They will set the standards and operating principles that will be used to propel the team forward. They will also form the foundation for shifting how people work. Although you will want the team to adhere to the existing corporate values, they will draw strength from the team values. Ensure that team values and organizational values are closely aligned. Share them with the CEO and sponsor, get their feedback and be sure they are comfortable with them.

You will want to develop values that are more in alignment with an entrepreneurial culture. Even though there is a proliferation of information on team-building and high-performance teams, there is less understanding of the importance of values on entrepreneurial behavior.

Get the team actively involved in developing and defining the values that they feel are important. Provide examples and clear explanations of what they mean. These values should be personal and professional. Individuals will want an opportunity to identify those values that are important to them personally. The values should also reflect the way team members will interact with one another, the rest of the organization, and customers. Team values will be put to the test during the more challenging times. They will influence decision-making and how the team deals with conflicts.

There are numerous values you will want to include, but here are a few to consider:

- Accountability

- Listening

- Learning

- Creativity

- Decisiveness

- Knowledge-sharing

- Self-responsibility

- Risk-taking

- Resourcefulness

- Responsiveness, and

- Collaboration.

Clearly articulating these values is important. Calling attention to them when they are ignored is just as important.

Values will define the group. Living by the values will demonstrate their worth.

Are values an integral part of your team-building process?

_____

Which team values do you think are most important?

_____

6.4 Stretching People

Corporate entrepreneurs who sign up for new initiatives want to learn and grow. One of the fastest ways to stretch them is to move them outside their comfort zone. They need an opportunity to try new things in a safe environment to gain a sense of confidence and accomplishment. This helps them take on more responsibilities and drives increases in productivity. They will be able to get more done when they step outside their comfort zone. *Taking people outside of their comfort zone helps them grow faster.*

If you've been in an organization for a number of years, you have a pretty good sense of what will fly and what won't. You've probably been down a million dead ends trying to do something new that just didn't seem to work. Or you may have tried or suggested something different that got shot down for not being the "company way." Unfortunately, these situations have created limits to your thinking. They prevent you from thinking outside of the box. The longer you've been with a company, the more you know about what won't work than what will. All of these experiences stop you from thinking beyond what you know and doing things that might make a difference.

There is great comfort in sticking with what you know. There is the illusion that you have more control if things remain the same. Why rock the boat? Moving outside one's comfort zone is fraught with potential minefields. For a corporate entrepreneur, the opposite is true. You see moving outside your comfort zone as an opportunity to learn, to grow, and to push the limits of your own capabilities. You understand that the real value is in the experience and what you learn from it.

The vice president of human resources for a major management consulting firm was intrigued with one resume that stood out among the thousands of resumes the company received each week. He invited the candidate in for an interview. Once the candidate was in front of him, he asked, "Why would someone in your position in one of the top Fortune 100 companies give up a good salary, bonus, stock options and bright future to start your own firm?" The candidate looked across the room to an empty chair and said, "I just needed to find out what I knew and what I didn't. Then I knew." This individual was willing to step outside his comfort zone. He had been a corporate entrepreneur and wanted to find out if he could transfer those skills to being an entrepreneur.

It is important to test the limits of your own capabilities. Only when you push the limits of what you know and step outside of your comfort zone can you see what is possible. It also helps you understand what you don't know and what you need to learn. Find ways to enable individuals to step up to the table and stretch.

If you are stretching people, you are empowering them. It helps keep them motivated and energized. Delegation and empowerment are intertwined. The more you delegate, the more empowered the team will become.

Is there a concerted effort in your organization to stretch and grow people?

_____

What are you doing to empower people?

_____

6.5 Lead By Following

Delegating control to the team members keeps things moving. The delegation of authority and control to the team makes them accountable for their actions. Often, decisions must be made on the fly to keep things moving and the team must take responsibility for and ownership of those decisions. That's not to say that you want to turn over control of the project, but certain decisions should be made by the team. A leader is often more effective when he or she *leads by following*.

A critical part of developing a new business, product, or service is keeping an open mind to the various options that present themselves to you. It is not surprising to see how often the initial specifications for a product change dramatically when the product/service is actually delivered. The team usually has the best grasp of the changing customer requirements, and it makes sense that they be actively involved in adjusting the product requirements.

Problems arise that may require detailed knowledge of the situation and need immediate attention. The leader can provide an opinion, but may not have enough information to make the best decision. More often than not, the team has a better sense of what needs to get done and the best way to do it. You want the team to keep pushing the edge of the envelope. Until they feel empowered to push forward, they will hold back from making bold decisions. It is the bold decisions that provide the greatest leaps forward.

The true test for you as a leader will be stepping outside of your own comfort zone and letting other people lead the way. Leading by following is a management philosophy designed to develop the leadership skills of team members and a way for leaders to learn and grow. Leading by following will open new vistas. It will enable you to see the project in an entirely different light. It will expand your concept of what is possible and it will provide you with new insight that will be useful in making better decisions.

As a leader, you need to have enough trust in yourself to let go of making all the decisions. Even when you don't have all the facts, you sometimes just have to take a leap of faith. Take calculated risks and delegate decision-making to the team when it makes sense. Delegating decision-making to the team forces everyone to be an active participant in the decision process.

As a team member, you will experience what it is like to make the tough calls. Not only will you have to live with your decisions, you will have to answer to the team. Making the right decision is worth as much as making a decision. Too often, projects get bogged down by the inability to make a decision.

Leading by following is a management style that will not make sense for everyone. Figure out the best way to delegate control and authority. You want to move forward as quickly and effectively as possible. Letting others lead may pave the way for that to happen.

As a leader, do you lead by following or use traditional management practices?

_____

As a team member, are you given the opportunity to make some of the tough decisions?

_____

6.6 Tell Us What to Do

At times, the team will defer to the leader to make decisions faster. Despite the fact that you want to empower people, there are times when the team wants the leader to make the decision. It may be something that they don't feel comfortable with, there may be a disagreement among team members about what to do, or it may be a decision they don't feel qualified to make. There is also an element of risk in some decisions. Trying to reach a consensus may just get in the way. It is better to have the team say *tell us what to do* than to struggle with making a decision.

This is not a reflection on the team's ability to reach a decision; it is often an indication that they need a quick decision to move forward. Being decisive and making timely decisions is critical. You may want to establish some guidelines regarding the types of decisions that require senior management approval and a process for how major decisions are made. The following chart is an example of how you can set up a framework for decision making that will help the team make decisions.

Decision Making Framework

Alignment With Goals	Market Attractiveness	Business Impact	Project Impact	Company Capability	Support
Strategic Fit	Real Market Opportunity	Increase in Revenue or Profitability	Impact On: • Time • Cost • Quality	Leverage Core Competencies	Champion
Aligned With Priorities	Adds Customer Value	Cross Functional Impact	Trade-offs	Resource Availability	Level of Influence
Measurable Outcome	Gives Competitive Advantage	Costs	Resources Requirements	Funding Requirements	Sufficient Resources
	Long range Outlook	Short and Long term Results		ROI	Commitment

Source: Adapted from Michael Treacy

Entrepreneurial risk holds both an element of loss and an opportunity for gain. As a leader, you may be willing to make the tough calls, but the team may not. Learning to manage risk effectively can help the team mitigate risk, reduce losses and leverage gains. Risk-taking is a key component of any new initiative, so taking risks will be a major part of the job. The key is taking calculated risks.

A corporate entrepreneur will weigh the upside and downside of any risk before making a decision. Calculated risk-takers know going in the probabilities behind each decision. Find individuals on the team who are calculated risk-takers and give them the freedom to make some of the tough calls. You can involve those who are not risk-takers in the risk management process by having them identify and prioritize project risks at the start of the project. Have them work on identifying risk drivers and assessing the probabilities and severity of the risks on project plans. Getting them involved up front will help the team understand the importance of risk management to the overall project.

When the team defers to the leader, it may be because they don't trust themselves to make the right decision. As the leader, you must help them build trust in themselves.

Does your decision-making process hinder or support new initiatives?

_____

Are you comfortable delegating decision-making?

_____

Are you a calculated risk-taker?

_____

6.7 Two Days in Woods

Spending a couple of days in the woods with a new team is a terrific way to get people to value differences and create new bonds. Although your team might think you are crazy when you suggest taking them to the woods, don't be dissuaded. If senior management questions your judgment on this one, stand your ground. Two days in the woods can create a high-performance team more quickly than all the internal team-building exercises you could dream of. *Nature provides a forum for building a high performance team.*

Often you are putting together teams of highly intelligent people who are used to being individual contributors. They have probably spent a good part of their career striving to be high achievers to get ahead. This might have been good when being an individual contributor was the best way to climb the corporate ladder, but times have changed. Building high-performance teams that work together to achieve results is what is required. Two days in the woods is a quick way to break old habits.

One corporate entrepreneur took a team of six individual contributors who were extremely talented, highly educated top performers to the woods for two days of team building. They were young, smart, and convinced that the leader had lost his mind. Each was determined to outshine the others. They started on some easy team-building exercises and then approached a wooden beam that was suspended 20 feet off the ground. The goal was to walk across the beam without falling. The hotshot of the group raised his hand to go first and did it quite effortlessly. Then the leader asked the instructor for a blindfold and things got interesting. Suddenly, the administrative support person asked for the blindfold and said she was going to climb the 50-foot pole blindfolded and walk across the wire at the top. This leveled the playing field in an instant.

Throughout the two days, the team took on team challenges and found that breaking course records was more important than competing with one another. In two days they had created an effective team able and willing to attack any challenge put in front of them. Back at the office, they translated what they had learned into practice. In fact, they were the ones who said they wanted to shorten staff meetings to 20 minutes, because they felt that they had more productive ways to spend time and 20 minutes was more than enough time. This team of six people grew the business 75 percent the first year and they were the fastest-growing group in the company. Going to the woods for two days made a big difference.

Building high-performance teams starts with understanding the individual characteristics and personalities of team members. Leverage personality and behavioral assessment tools to make these visible. They accelerate the team's ability to see what needs to be changed. Unlearning old behaviors and learning new ones needs to happen quickly, and this is a fast way to start. Team-building exercises are another.

You will want to find creative ways to tear down old behaviors and build new ones. People don't like to change, so you may have to force that change for it to happen in a time frame that makes sense for your project.

What are you doing to create high-performance teams?

6.8 Getting Unstuck

There are times during a project when the team actually gets depressed and negative about their progress. Tempers are short, there is a lack of tolerance for each other, and there is a rash of finger-pointing. This is often a sign that the team is stuck. They are not sure which way to turn or what to do next. You can feel the tension in the air. Having a meeting will only fuel the flames of anger and frustration. Breaking the tension and getting to the root cause is essential. Sitting down with everyone individually is the best way to let them vent, and bringing along a bag of M&Ms can help. *Dealing with conflict and tension is critical to getting unstuck.*

As the project evolves, individual frustrations gradually build and many team members will keep them bottled up inside. The outward signs of frustration are evident to everyone, but no one is quite sure what is triggering the tension. Team members often feel that they've had to leave their own individual needs on the back burner in support of the team. They have reached a point where they need to vent their frustration. As the leader, you are the only one who can listen to each one of them and get them to see what is happening.

Listening and empathy are two key competencies you will want to have. Sitting down with someone to listen to their concerns and frustrations may be all that is needed to make them feel better, and candy makes things a little sweeter. The candy isn't what is important—it's the sharing and caring that make a difference. It is often helpful to pull the team together after you've met with everyone individually and help them understand that everyone is feeling the same way. Emphasize that they are all in this boat together. Just listening is not enough; having empathy and a clear understanding of the emotional makeup of the team will ensure that you can get through these times with the least amount of disruption.

In one situation, it was clear that the team was feeling the resentment and isolation from the rest of the organization. The team did not realize the extent to which the rest of the organization resented them. They were the rising star. They were getting the funding and resources they needed. The rest of the company was not. Seeing the problem more clearly helped them understand the other side and enabled them to deal with it more effectively.

Dealing head-on with conflict minimizes disruptions. Conflict management is another core competency that will be required by you and key individuals on your team. Avoiding conflict only slows things down. Conflict can be destructive or healthy. Foster an environment where differences can be shared openly and discussed freely. Find the right balance of empathy and directness to minimize the emotional dramas that will unfold. Refine your conflict management skills. Fight for what is right.

Are listening and empathy key competencies in your organization?

_____

How does your organization deal with conflict and tension?

_____

6.9 Struggle for Legitimacy

Even though the CEO and corporation have sanctioned the new initiative, the rest of the organization may be slow to embrace it. The organization may understand the need for the new initiative intellectually, but often they can't accept it emotionally. By its very nature a new business initiative, product, or service consumes precious resources and introduces changes that threaten the stability of the existing organization. As a result you may find that you are *swimming upstream* against an entrenched culture that does not welcome the change.

Establishing legitimacy is part of the process and part of the problem. On one hand, you realize that you need the cooperation and support of other parts of the organization to accomplish your objectives. On the other hand, you realize that the rest of the organization may be silently hoping that you fail, so cooperation is slow and painful. The trick is to find ways to deal with the resistance that will inevitably arise when you are trying to establish legitimacy for your project and your people.

The best way to establish legitimacy is to get traction and show momentum. Often the very fact that you are making progress gets others to understand that you are going to do this with or without them. Eventually they begin to realize that the probability of this initiative succeeding is increasing, and their initial resistance may be viewed negatively. In other situations you will need the political clout of the sponsor or CEO.

Recognize that it is often necessary to find viable alternatives to support your efforts, even if it requires going outside the organization. Always factor this into your planning. This may not be standard practice within your organization, so include it when establishing parameters with sponsors and the CEO.

The team must do its part in establishing legitimacy as well. Give them the tools and support to deal with resistance. Motivate the team to be creative about getting around organizational obstacles. They will need to challenge assumptions, suspend judgment and look for viable alternatives. The team will need to set the stage for collaboration.

Focus on developing competencies that will come in handy, like influence and negotiating skills. Influence will be the key to gaining acceptance of your ideas. Understanding the best way to influence different types of people is something you can learn. Knowing who the key players are that can influence the outcome may be just as important. Negotiating for a firmly held position may be difficult if the organization has not embraced what you are doing. You may find that you are not bargaining from a position of strength. Linking your position to broader organizational goals may help. Having good influencing and negotiating skills will be invaluable.

You will find that legitimacy alone is not enough. Gaining legitimacy is the first step to acceptance and support. Expectations will have to be met to preserve and sustain legitimacy over time.

What obstacles have you encountered when trying to establish legitimacy?

_____

What creative steps have you taken to establish legitimacy?

_____

SUMMARY: Chapter 6: Engage Teams So They Thrive— *Team Dynamics*

Entrepreneurial initiatives create a unique set of team dynamics. The chaotic and uncertain nature of these initiatives places increased demands on team members. On the surface, being part of an entrepreneurial team is inviting and looks like a lot of fun. The reality is that it involves a tremendous amount of work and stress. Individuals who sign up for these types of initiatives don't always understand how grueling they can be. Experienced corporate entrepreneurs, on the other hand, thrive and are energized by such projects. Creating a highly productive team requires an infrastructure to support them and the tools to enable them to work effectively.

The key is setting expectations up front to ensure that everyone is fully aware of what is involved in the project. Dealing with the highs and lows is extremely stressful. Because the team will be working in an environment full of ambiguity, it is essential that they clearly understand their roles and responsibilities. Roles and responsibilities identify who is responsible for what. Team values set the tone and establish parameters for the how the team will work together. Adhering to values keeps the team in alignment with the individual and collective needs of the group.

Stretch people outside their comfort zone. This will enable them to grow faster and be more productive sooner. Individuals need to expand their horizons, and moving outside their comfort zone helps them do that. Find creative ways to build a high-performing team. Leverage team-building exercises and get the team to see the value of team-work in getting things done. Use outside facilitators for team-building where appropriate.

Determine what level of control versus autonomy will be needed to keep things moving. Be sure that everyone is clear on who is responsible for making decisions and how decisions will be made. Decide on the best way to deal with conflict and tension among team members. Create rules for dealing with disputes and resolving issues quickly. Get the team to understand that they will be swimming upstream against an entrenched culture that may not embrace what they are doing.

Team dynamics play a pivotal role in moving a project forward.

Corporate Entrepreneur Insights and Lessons Learned

- Signing Up—"In the beginning everybody wants to be part of it because of the excitement. Once reality sets in, they can't get away fast enough."

- Team—"The team liked being part of a cause. It was a unique and valued opportunity for them to do something they believed in."

- Cause—"The project turns into a cause that you need to drive through to completion."

- Adrenaline Thing—"When you are working in a new product development environment, the excitement keeps you going. It is an adrenaline thing."

- Values—"There were no team values so it wasn't clear what values were driving the place. Everyone talked over one another in meetings and it wasn't clear exactly what we had accomplished when the meetings ended. It was very frustrating."

- Comfort Zone—"Corporate entrepreneurs are comfortable moving outside their comfort zone."

- Stretching—Stretching and enabling people to think and decide for themselves engages people in lively debates that are healthy."

- Persistence—"It takes persistence and diligence to make sure you've found the best way. It takes more time, but it saves you in the end."

- Right Behaviors—"Innovate ways to evaluate behaviors, because you need the right people with the right behaviors in the right places."

- Recruiting—"It was important to hire people who have an established record of innovation and can deal in the abstract."

- Stress—"I tried to manage stress by asking everyone to take one day to do something in their community. We also talked a lot about the need to manage our health, so informally each person had a goal to do something for their health."

- Career Enhancement—"The team members thought the role was career-enhancing until they found out how hard it was."

Chapter 7

Discover Ideas with Value

Creativity

7. 1 Exploration

Creativity refers to the process of creating new thoughts and ideas that become the fuel for innovation. The roots of creativity are found in psychology. In the past, the topic of creativity was not widely studied in psychology. A key reason may be its early association with mystical beliefs. It can be difficult to explore a subject that is not taken seriously or does not lend itself to scientific inquiry. But today creativity is being widely studied with a focus on its pragmatic ability to increase organizational creativity. *Creativity is the discovery of something new.*

The subject of creativity has been examined in numerous books, so we won't dwell on it here. Instead, we will look at aspects of creativity related to corporate entrepreneurs. This includes the internal processes more closely associated with thoughts, beliefs, and emotions, and the role of diversity in creating a whole brain that can generate ideas with business value. We'll also look at the need to stimulate creative thought through collaboration, and the desire to understand what inspires people to be creative and entrepreneurial.

Creativity is a process and an outcome. The process refers to the various ways individuals use their thinking skills to approach problems. It includes things like experimentation, out-of-the-box thinking, imagination, dealing with ambiguity, and exploring the unknown. It refers to the process of relating seemingly unrelated things. The outcome of creativity is to develop ideas that have business value or to solve complex and challenging business problems. It is both an internal and external process.

Internally, it is a cognitive process that leverages a person's experiences, memory, and perception of things. It is part of the analytical process used to make decisions. Creativity involves heuristics, which is not well understood. Heuristics is a particular technique for learning, discovery and problem-solving that is not based on algorithms. There are no rules or formulas that guide creative thinking. Creative people develop a unique way of processing and assimilating information.

Externally, creativity is related to the social and cultural environment. The right environment provides the motivation for creativity. Research has shown that creativity can be linked to specific variables associated with an environment, including role models, resources, and culture. These factors can determine the level of creativity and adoption of it throughout an organization. There is some thought that the proper environment can foster creativity in everyone. The research has tended to look at the internal and external process of creativity separately, without combining them into a total picture. Both processes are required to support and encourage creativity in an organization.

Creativity is a process of thought, belief, and emotions. It is simple yet complex. Once you get a thought, you develop it into a more complete thought or idea. If you believe in your idea and you put emotion behind it, then you can manifest it into something. All three of these work in unison and must be in complete alignment. If you have a thought and believe it will work, but don't put the emotion or energy into it then it won't. If any one of these pieces is missing, it doesn't work. Creativity in organizations works the same way.

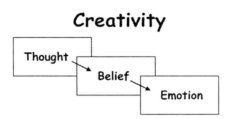

For creativity to flourish, you must nurture the internal and external process of creation. Thought, belief, and emotions are the key components that will enable your people to generate and cultivate new ideas. Creativity is not something that you can turn on or off like a switch. It is a reflective and internal process that can often only be achieved through an activity that creates an environment for creative thought. Creating an environment for creativity will help foster that creativity.

Ideas alone are not enough. The key is having ideas that are practical, that can be implemented, and that generate profitable revenue for the organization. Organizations are full of people with new and innovative ideas. Your challenge is finding the ideas that make sense.

Creativity is the fuel that drives innovation.

What is behind your organization's desire to be more creative?

7.2 Gateway

As a corporate entrepreneur, you may be required to pass through a gateway to the right side of your brain—the part of the brain that is creative, artistic, and musical. Right-brain thinkers are more holistic and intuitive. They are good at integrating and synthesizing things. Left-brain thinkers are more analytical and logical. They are more sequential in their thinking, quantitative, fact-based, and detail-oriented. Most people have a left or right brain dominance. The difference is in how their brain processes information. *Creativity requires finding the gateway to the right side of the brain.*

Creative people are highly intelligent and enjoy searching for something new. Their personality and social style play a part in their creativity. They have an inherent impulse to learn. They enjoy the process of discovery. They are good problem-solvers. Individuals who are highly creative are independent thinkers and confident, and enjoy complexity and risk-taking.

The right side of the brain provides the right context for creativity. It is fertile ground for creative thinking because it is unencumbered by logic, judgment, or rules. It is the area of the brain which generates creative thoughts that eventually manifest themselves into new product and service ideas. Right-brain thinkers will process information very rapidly, often in a nonlinear and non-sequential way. They can relate disparate ideas and thoughts. They easily see spatial relationships.

Right-brain thinkers can deal effectively with complexity. They can see how an idea fits into the bigger picture. They are more eager to experience things through sight, touch or feelings. They use intuition to influence and guide their decision-making process. They are more visual and want to create a mental picture of the idea to ground it in their thinking.

Left-brain thinkers are usually strong planners, more organized, focused and detail-oriented. They are not easily distracted and are usually good at time management. They will plan their work and work their plan. They will use logic and reasoning to make decisions. They are task-oriented and prefer working with a clear set of instructions. As corporate entrepreneurs they are very good at getting things done and bringing things to closure.

Entrepreneurs are thought to be more right brain-oriented, although there has been limited research with corporate entrepreneurs. Corporate entrepreneurs need to have the qualities of both right—and left-brain thinkers. They need to operate in a more balanced way. As a leader, you will need to leverage the creativity of right-brain thinkers and the analytical thinking of left-brain thinkers.

Although you will want both right—and left-brain thinkers on your team, you must create an environment that enables everyone to tap into the right side of their brain.

What are you doing to create an environment where individuals can be creative?

7.3 Meditation

Creative individuals have their own thought process. They process information by looking at similarities and differences. They relate information into constructs and structures that they perceive are in harmony. They have an ability to eliminate extraneous information that gets in their way. They form a total picture of what they see into a vision. They use various methods to generate new thinking. Meditation is just one of the ways they create an environment for creative thinking. *Thoughts and ideas are developed in the void.*

The void refers to something that is empty, vacant, containing nothing. Creative individuals create something out of nothing. Think of a time when you tried to remember something or someone, but the harder you tried, the harder it was to remember. Once you let go of thinking about it, the answer would pop into your head. This is the same type of experience. It is in the empty space between your thoughts where creative ideas are formed. Meditation and running are two ways of triggering that mental state.

Transcendental meditation (TM) has been around for decades, but only in the last ten years have physicians studied the effects of TM on the body and mind. As a practice, it is a good way to reduce stress, re-energize yourself, or relax. It slows down all of your body's processes, including your mind. Everyone has their own way of slowing their mind down. Runners say that running helps them clear their heads and think more clearly. Some individuals get their inspiration from nature. It helps them to not only solve problems but to envision new ideas. Others may prefer to brainstorm in small groups to get the ideas flowing.

Creativity

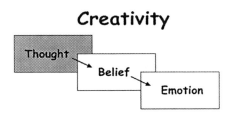

A senior consultant with a prestigious management consulting firm would stop every day at two-thirty in the afternoon to meditate. He would meditate right there in his office with the door closed and a sign posted on his door. At first his colleagues thought it was very strange, until they understood what he was doing. He was creating an environment in which he could think about problems and situations with his clients. These daily meditations were well-known and even sanctioned by upper management. Everyone knew not to disturb this man when the sign was on his door. He used this opportunity re-energize himself physically and mentally. A wealth of ideas streamed forth from this twenty-minute break each afternoon.

You may not want to go as far as having your team meditate each day, because meditation is just one of the ways people generate their best thinking. The point is that you need to create an environment where creative thinking can occur. Working twelve hours a day does not leave a lot of room for creativity. You probably have a few team members who are runners and you wouldn't stop them from running at lunch, so why stop someone from meditating?

In this fast-paced world, doesn't twenty minutes of quiet time meditating, running, or communing with nature sound good? Find ways to stimulate creative thinking to generate new ideas.

Is your organization open to allowing people time for creative thinking?

_____

What ways do you use to stimulate creative thinking?

_____

7.4 Conviction

Belief in an idea is what gives it life. It grounds it. A belief is a something that you have confidence in and you trust. If you believe in something, you have a conviction that it is true. Like thinking, belief is an internal process that takes root in your mind and gut. Believing in something does not make it true, but it provides the context for making it come true. A firm conviction will be needed as you move your idea forward. If you do not believe in it, you will not convince others of its worthiness. *Belief in your idea is a key part of making it so.*

An idea that is grounded in belief has a longer shelf life than one that doesn't. It buys you time to determine if the idea has merit. It helps you find the information you will need to convince others that your idea is worthy. Belief is what will connect you to the right people, resources, and situations that confirm or dismiss what you are doing.

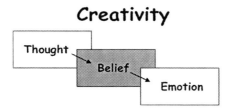

Getting others to believe in your idea is what is ultimately important. The more people who believe in the idea, the more momentum you will build around it. People will provide additional input that will mold and shape the idea into something bigger and better. As they do, their belief in the idea will grow.

An organization is more likely to invest in something that the CEO and senior management believe in. They will want supporting data to convince them that it has merit. Even though you may have put together a convincing business case for the idea on paper, it will be their belief in the idea that will make the difference. The rest of the organization will follow their lead. Belief alone can take an idea farther than you would imagine. Eventually, belief in the ideas is transferred to a belief in you.

Belief and doubt are two sides of the same coin. Belief and conviction are a powerful force that will attract others to your idea. Doubt will do just the reverse.

Is there a strong belief in your initiative?

7.5 Passion

Emotions provide the fuel, the energy that turns the idea into something. Most external entrepreneurs are passionate about what they are doing. They draw strength from their belief in what they are doing, but they move forward because of their passion for what they are doing. It is no different here. You can have many good ideas and people can believe in them, but if you don't have someone with the passion to drive them, they will go nowhere. Corporate entrepreneurs are passionate about what they do. *Emotion is what propels the idea forward.*

The organization must also be passionate about the idea for it to move forward. There must be a common feeling within the organization that what you are doing is right. If it is in alignment with the strategic direction of the company, then you will find the emotional support you need from senior management. If it is not, then it will be more challenging to obtain and maintain support over time.

Creativity

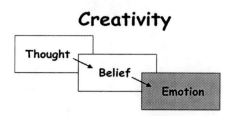

The emotional support you receive will give your idea more validity and forward motion. Emotions and passions are a form of energy. Like a magnet, the energy can either have a positive or negative charge. Positive charges are attracted to positive charges and negative to negative. Emotions can be negative or positive as well. If you think about your emotions in this way, you can begin to see the importance of having the right emotions and energy behind your idea. There is an interesting process that seems to attract people together—the law of attraction.

The Law of Attraction is a book by Michael Losier, an expert on Neuro Linguistic Programming. The premise of his book is that each of us is like a magnet that gives off vibrations, either positive or negative. The law of attraction will respond to whatever vibration you are giving, good or bad. If you believe strongly in something and are excited about it, you are giving off a positive charge. People with the same level of vibration will be naturally attracted to one another. You will be surprised how easily you are attracted to the right people, information, and resources. This helps you to move the idea forward.

Of course, having a CEO who is passionate about a new initiative is your best bet. The CEO can harness the support you will need, whether the rest of the organization buys into it or not. The CEO will also have a vested interest in seeing that it succeeds. A sponsor should be as passionate as you are about the new initiative. A sponsor who is actively involved but not emotionally invested is less likely to give you the level of support you might need. Emotions are what bind us to something.

Not everyone on the team will have the same passion. The idea people are usually the most passionate. They love seeing their idea turn into something tangible.

Unfortunately, they are not always the same ones who make it happen. The individuals who stay late and work long hours are also highly passionate about what they are doing. They are driven to see the initiative succeed. They are willing to do what it takes. You will need to manage their enthusiasm, for they are the ones most likely to burn out.

Not everyone will be passionate about what you are doing. Leverage those who are. Passion is something that team members will acquire over time as they get more involved in understanding the value of the idea.

Are you passionate about what you are doing?

_____

How passionate is the team and the rest of the organization?

_____

7.6 Whole Brain

Creative ideas have no value unless they make sense. It requires a whole brain to determine the worthiness and value of an idea. There will never be a shortage of ideas, just an inability to chase after all of them. Creativity is a right-brain function but validating creative ideas is a left-brain function. Leveraging the right and left side of the brain is what is needed to rationalize those ideas and determine their viability in the market, strategically, financially and technically. Finding someone who can do both is a challenge. Putting together a group that can do both is not. *It takes a diverse group to represent a whole brain.*

Whole brain means more than using both sides of your brain. It refers to the ability to use all four quadrants of your brain. The concept of whole brain was developed by Ned Hermann, creator of the Hermann Brain Dominance Instrument (HBDI). It is a cognitive assessment tool that looks at the four quadrants of your brain and how you use each part to perform various functions, from administrative work to intuitive thinking. Cognitive abilities are the thinking and problem-solving styles of people. The four quadrants of the brain are described in the graphic below.

Hermann Brain Dominance Profile

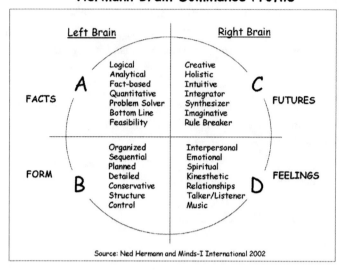

Source: Ned Hermann and Minds-I International 2002

According to Sheri Woods Green of Minds-I International, left-brain thinkers in quadrant A are into facts and figures, while those in B are into processes and systems, those in C are visionary and entrepreneurial, and those in D are relationship-minded. Individuals in each quadrant not only think differently, they prefer to receive information in different forms, and they process information differently to make decisions.

Anyone who scores high in all four quadrants would be functioning as a whole brain. Only a small fraction of individuals operate fully on all four cylinders. So it makes sense that it takes a diverse group to represent a fully functioning brain, a whole brain.

Validating a new idea requires a whole brain but it doesn't just refer to cognitive thinking styles. It also means drawing upon a diverse group of skills. Putting together a diverse group of people from various disciplines with different skills, personalities, thinking styles and experiences helps you create your own whole brain team.

Mix it up when it comes to putting your team together. New people bring a fresh perspective. They are not tainted by the existing culture. They don't have the organizational baggage that might stop others from pursuing a course of action. Radical thinkers stimulate the thinking process. They challenge the way you see things. Complainers can be annoying, but they may have some legitimate points that might help. People you don't really like may have something of value to contribute if you give them a chance. You will want a process for validating ideas, but you need a team with the breadth and depth to develop it into something worth investing in.

The more diverse the team, the more likely you are to develop an idea with value. It takes a diverse group to represent a fully functioning brain.

What does your organization do to create whole brain thinking?

---

7. 7 Team Sport

Creativity is an individual and organizational process, but it is also a team process. Not everyone on your team will be creative, but collectively all team members can contribute to turning the idea into a reality. So make idea generation a team sport where everyone gets a chance to weigh in on the idea. Chances are that the idea will be more realistic and more viable once the team gets finished with it. Doing this also serves to get everyone committed to the idea if you decide to move forward. *Creativity is a team sport where everyone makes a contribution.*

Building a cross-functional team that focuses on creativity is a great way to accelerate idea generation. Some organizations are developing "idea factories" where groups converge to develop new ideas. Although some research suggests that typical brainstorming sessions are not the best way to generate creativity, having a cross-functional team evaluate ideas can be a good way to distinguish ideas with value from those without value. Individuals need time to reflect and generate new ideas, but they also need the opportunity to test their ideas. There is no better way to do so than to bring those ideas to the team.

Creative thinking is stimulated when you combine it with enjoyable activities. Sitting in a conference room, staring at a white board is not the most inspirational activity for generating new thinking. Changing the environment changes the context for creative thinking. Participating in something fun helps you clear your mind. Both are necessary for creative thinking. A major financial institution took their team ice skating at Rockefeller center to clear their heads, another company did a scavenger hunt to get closer to potential customers. You may want to allow people to meet regularly for idea generation sessions. Or you may want to give them incentives to come up with new ideas, then fund the best ideas.

Hewlett-Packard has a separate fund that is given to groups that come up with innovative ideas. 3M gives their employees the ability to spend fifteen percent of their working hours on new ideas. Be sure that you are serious about raising the level of creativity in your organization, or it could backfire. It is like having a suggestion box but not doing anything with the suggestions. Individuals will want to see some of their ideas funded or, at the least, taken into consideration for funding.

As with any other team sport, you must practice as a team before you can get good at what you are doing. The more individuals openly share their ideas among their peers, the more quickly you will see new energy and excitement build. Getting people conditioned to start thinking outside the box is an excellent way to increase the organization's creativity.

Creative thinking is an internal process. Developing creativity is an external process. Making it a team activity helps you combine the two.

Does your organization view creativity as a team sport?

7.8 Camp Fire

Creativity requires inspiration. People must be motivated and inspired to be creative. They want to understand why someone believes in an idea or why someone else is so passionate about it. It is human nature to want to know. Sharing those beliefs and passions is a way to inspire others, make them more creative, or get them to take on new challenges. *Sitting around a camp fire can provide the right environment for inspiration.*

For one entrepreneurial team, a camp fire at night in the woods provided that inspiration. It was the first night of an off-site meeting at a conference center in the woods. After a long day of working, the team found a fire pit out in the woods and built a fire that lasted late into the night. They took the opportunity to get to know each other on a different level. There was something sacred, ancient, and profound about it. The ambiance of the cool night and warm fire probably inspired the bonding of souls that occurred that night.

The team had found an almost sacred environment in which they could reflect and express their hopes and concerns for the journey they had elected to take together. That night they shared their personal and professional concerns with one another. They got to understand people's drive and motivation for wanting to get involved in such a risky endeavor. Each had their own personal and professional reasons for joining the team. Sharing those reasons with everyone created a spiritual bond between them. They were more willing to freely share their thoughts, beliefs and emotions. They were laying the groundwork for being more creative as a team.

The camp fire created a spiritual bond which took the team to a new level of performance. They began to see the project in a new light, which helped them realize the value each person brought to the table. It helped reignite their creativity and generated a whole new set of ideas about what other things they could be doing. They brought those ideas and their excitement back to the project. You may choose a figurative version of the camp fire experience instead, but you will want to find ways to inspire and motivate your people.

One night by an open fire lit the sparks for new list of creative ideas that carried the team through to the end. Perhaps it was the setting or just the opportunity for the team to look at the situation in a new light, but it made a difference. Never underestimate the opportunity to stimulate creativity in the most unexpected places.

What are you doing to inspire people to be creative?

_____

SUMMARY: Chapter 7: Discover Ideas with Value—*Creativity*

Creativity is one of the key building blocks of corporate entrepreneurship; it's the idea generation part. Creativity is rooted in psychology and has only recently been studied from a pragmatic perspective. It is both an internal and external process. Internally, it is an individual thought process. Externally, it is the way an organization sets up an environment to stimulate creativity. Creativity itself is a process of thought, belief, and emotion. Once you have a thought you must believe in it, and then put emotion behind it to materialize it. Creativity is simple yet complex.

As a building block, creativity is all about the exploration and discovery of new ideas. It requires leveraging the right side of the brain, the part of the brain that is creative, artistic, and musical. The environment must be right for creativity to flourish. New ideas are created in a void. Thinking too hard clutters the mind and leaves no room for creativity. Meditation, running, or a walk in the woods frees the mind and creates the void from which thoughts and ideas can emerge.

Thoughts alone are not enough—having a strong belief and conviction in your idea is what helps make it so. Belief is a key determinant for convincing others that the idea has merit and value. A strong belief enables you to attract and gather information to support what you believe. Emotion provides the energy that propels the idea forward. Energy and passion are what give the idea life and momentum. There are plenty of ideas, but the real challenge is sorting out which ones have value. It takes a whole brain to validate an idea. Right-brain thinkers are good at coming up with ideas, left-brain thinkers excel at analyzing the ideas' merits.

Creativity is a team sport where everyone should be actively involved. Not everyone can generate great ideas, but they can participate in evaluating and enhancing them. Leverage the skills of the team to identify, develop, and evaluate ideas. Never underestimate the value of inspiration in getting individuals to come up with new and better ideas. They need a reason and a place to be inspired. Find creative ways to inspire people.

Creativity provides the fuel for innovation.

Corporate Entrepreneur Insights and Lessons Learned

- Creativity—"There are those who love the creative process. The more they do it, the more they want to do it."

- Idea Person—"An idea person thrives in environment of change but gets bored easily."

- Concept Champion—"The idea itself gives you the courage, the permission to go beyond what you think you are capable of doing."

- New Space—"The dynamics of this new space began to infiltrate the rest of the organization and demonstrated how work can be fun and rewarding at the same time. We were more creative in the new environment."

- Believing—"Believing in the concept made it easier to convince others of its value."

- Belief—"The team was made up mostly of women who were intense, incredibly bright, and well-educated. They were totally passionate about what they were doing. It was intimidating. Passion and belief in what they were doing was the fuel that drove them."

- Independent Thinking—"The development lab group thought differently than the traditional lines of business. They wanted to do intelligent concept testing instead of traditional focus groups. This enabled us to zero in on real customer needs."

- Artificial World—"We needed to replicate the real world to test and validate new product ideas with customers. So we created an artificial world that looked like the inside of the bank and hired actors to be bankers."

- Managing Passion—"Corporate entrepreneurs are passionate about their work and have more emotional swings. You need to nurture creative people, provide one-on-one coaching and give them extra TLC (tender loving care)."

- Mix of People—"Having a mix of internal and external people on the team shook things up and got us to think outside the box."

- Fun—"It was important to bring the whole team together twice a year and have fun. One year we skated in Rockefeller center, another we had a martini party."

- Bonding—"A bonding occurs that goes beyond words, an emotional experience that is personally rewarding."

Chapter 8

Lead the Way with Experimentation

Innovation

8.1   Extension Cord—the innovation should be *linked* back to the mother ship

8.2   Mother of Invention—*experimentation* helps perfect the innovation process

8.3   Lowest Common Denominator—resist *compromising* creativity out of your idea

8.4   Resisting Temptation—resist the temptation to *imitate* a competitor

8.5   Starting with a Blank Page—don't be afraid to *create* a new market

8.6   Balancing Act—find the right *balance* of risk and innovation

8.7   Value Creation—both internal and external innovations create *value*

8.8   Measures and Metrics—traditional *value drivers* are not enough

Corporate Entrepreneur Insights and Lessons Learned

8.1 Extension Cord

The roots of innovation are in technology, but innovation today is much more than that. Innovation has many definitions and like corporate entrepreneurship, there is no common definition. We'll use the following definition:

> Innovation is the integration of new and creative ideas
> into products, services, processes and practices.

There is plenty of information available on incremental and radical innovation, so we won't discuss it in depth here. In this chapter we'll look at innovation from a corporate entrepreneur's perspective.

As organizations invest in organic growth, it is important that their innovations have close ties to the core business. You can think of it as having an extension cord back to the organization. Straying too far afield from the core business is often a recipe for disaster. An organization that is transitioning to a culture of innovation may prefer to focus initially on incremental innovations and evolve to more radical innovations as it develops a track record of success. *Either way, the innovation should be linked back to the mother ship.*

Making investments in businesses more closely aligned with the core business is a viable first step on your way to building an innovative company. It also begins to condition the organization to the reality of what it will take to move into riskier investments in the future. Radical innovation should ultimately be the end goal, but not when you are getting started. The most innovative companies have worked hard to institutionalize innovation in their culture.

Recognizing the need to develop more innovative products, a large pharmaceutical company looked at the feasibility of setting up an innovation center. They identified an individual with a track record of being a change agent to evaluate the situation and set the stage for the change. This individual outlined the infrastructure and processes that would be required, and hired the entrepreneurial leader to lead the effort.

The goal was to create an environment for generating product ideas for new growth markets. The objective was to create new products from scratch that were outside the scope of the core lines of business. Funding for the innovation center came from each of the divisions. Each division had to reduce their own budget and eliminate resources to fund this effort. This of course created tremendous pressure for the entrepreneurial leader and team to perform.

Creating new products from scratch forced the team to work longer and harder to find high-value products. The entrepreneurial leader felt that he had to hit a home run right away to prove that the investment in the innovation center was worthwhile. The leader would have preferred to have had an opportunity to demonstrate a few short-term wins, singles, doubles, or triples by developing products more closely tied to existing lines of business. He felt that this would have kept the interest and commitment level higher. Ideally, he would have preferred corporate funding.

The innovation center was handicapped by not being able to touch existing products. Eventually, the innovation center developed a number of successful products, but also began developing extensions of existing product lines. The organization found it beneficial to use the innovation center to develop product line extensions. They also realized they had the capabilities to develop brand-new products from scratch with the right commitment of time, resources, funding, and leadership.

Keeping innovations tied to the core business helps minimize risks because you are able to leverage the organization's resources and intellectual capital. You can also create incremental value for the organization and the company's existing clients. This strategy lets you achieve greater acceptance of the innovation, and allows you to gain confidence in your ability to innovate and manage risk to take on bigger or more innovative projects over time. It also enables you to leverage the brand equity that exists with the core business.

Being linked to the core business provides a mechanism for keeping the innovation alive.

Are your innovations linked to the core business?

8.2 Experimentation is the Mother of Invention

The more innovation projects you do, the better you will get at doing them. Just like learning to ride a bike, the more you do it, the more comfortable and confident you get. It is the same with creating innovations. Like anything else, you must go through the process to understand what it is you don't know. On the surface, the concept of innovation seems simple and clear. It is the hidden barriers and obstacles that are hard to understand. *Experimentation helps perfect the innovation process.*

When you elect to become an innovative company, you wind up looking at the company in a new light. The systems that are the foundation of the core business often get in your way. People who are your top performers may not adapt well to a more entrepreneurial environment. The policies and procedures that made you efficient in the past can create obstacles. Your culture may be less agile and creative than it needs to be. The leadership may not be as collaborative or tolerant of ambiguity and failure.

These are the reasons why it is important to experiment. You will gradually come to see the change that will be required to move to a new paradigm, a new way of work that could potentially be 180 degrees from where it is today. It will take time to change the fundamental principles underlying your core business. So recognize this and accept it as part of the learning process. You will have to deal with all of these issues sooner or later, but trying to change them all at once can be disastrous.

The managing director of an executive education program on corporate entrepreneurship at a major university told a story about the process one organization went through as they transitioned to an innovation culture. As the company moved forward with their innovation program, they soon began to encounter one issue after another. One of the first problems they encountered was the compensation program. The company's incentive programs didn't support the new business model—in fact, they worked against it. Then they realized that the budgeting process got in the way, the financial systems were out of alignment, and so on. It is part of the learning process.

Only when you begin to experiment with innovation will you see which aspects of the core business do not support innovation. You may think you know this intuitively, but it isn't until you've been through the experience that you will understand the extent to which a system or process creates obstacles. Making them visible will be important to changing them for the next round of experimentation. The willingness to change processes and systems will illustrate an organization's flexibility, adaptability, and ability to embrace innovation.

There are limits to how far some organizations are willing to go to create a culture of innovation. Those organizations that stop short of experimenting with innovation will most likely be disappointed when they do. It is the experience itself that provides the learning and builds the competencies required to design, build, and implement new innovations successfully.

Are you experimenting with innovation, or are you jumping in with both feet?

8.3 Lowest Common Denominator

As you build an organization of creative thinkers, you will undoubtedly generate a wealth of new product, service, and business ideas. There is great value in having an organization that can work effectively to generate new ideas. For every idea you generate, you will have a thousand opinions about it. Unfortunately, it is not unusual to strip an idea of its creative value. You can compromise the creativity right out of an innovation and weaken the value of the final product. *Resist compromising creativity out of your ideas.*

Compromise is healthy, but it can also be dysfunctional. The kiss of death is compromising an idea and settling on the lowest common denominator. Find ways to ensure that some of your best thinking sticks to the original idea. As far-fetched as some of your ideas may seem, in reality the final idea will most likely turn out somewhere in between the original idea and a "realistic" one.

Senior management in particular may find some of the ideas preposterous or outrageous. Much of their thinking is still grounded in the core business, and seeing beyond that is often difficult. They will be thinking about minimizing risk or trying to determine if the innovation is in alignment with organizational goals. Some of their concerns will be valid, but others will be a reflection of their inability to see the same opportunity and value that you see. You will need to make the opportunity and value visible to them.

Creative ideas are not always welcomed. Look at all the skunkworks activity that gets started because senior management does not see the value at first. At 3M, one individual decided to continue working on his idea long after management told him to stop. If he hadn't gone ahead, we might not have Scotch Tape today.

One of the biggest challenges will be getting people to see the potential in your idea. They need to be educated and see what you already see. Find individuals who do not support what you are doing and ask them to explain why they don't support it. Do the same with those individuals who think it is a great idea. That way you get a healthy dose of reality. It helps you understand the objections and why some people can't see the value in the idea. Then you can determine if the value you see is real or not.

Customers are another barometer and an integral part of the innovation process. They provide valuable input into new product and service ideas. They can also take you off track. Some organizations that have relied on customers have found that it has taken them off track. Even the most innovative customers may not see the value in a new idea at first. Customer input should be weighed carefully when creating new innovations. Like your employees, they can comprise creativity out of new ideas.

Judgment can strip an idea of its potential value. It is natural to question and evaluate ideas that we can not visualize in our own minds. We are quick to make arbitrary judgments based on past experience or lack of evidence. Innovative ideas can easily fall into this trap. Suspending or deferring judgment can help keep innovation in ideas until you've had time to fully explore their worthiness. It is often easier to figure out why a creative idea won't work than to find reasons for why it will. Deferring judgment gives you the time to figure this out. Turn the tables and challenge the team to look for the reasons why it will work.

Do you compromise creativity out of your organization's ideas?

8.4 Resisting Temptation

The fast pace of change and increasing pressure from competitors makes imitating a competitor look like an easy choice. The temptation to imitate a competitor may be extremely strong, especially when you think of the risk and high costs of developing an original innovation. Unfortunately, product lifecycles are so short that it is increasingly difficult for an organization to gain and maintain a competitive advantage for long. Your competitor has already thought about what it will take to build the next version of their product or service. *Resist the temptation to imitate a competitor.*

Instead, leverage the marketing and education that they've already done in the market to solve a particular problem. Take advantage of the fact that your competitors have already paved the way, educated the market, and sold them on the idea. A major part of any new product introduction is the cost and effort associated with conditioning the market for a product. Explore markets that are already conditioned to buy. Leapfrog your competitors with a new version of the product.

A media company focused on the tradeshow industry saw an opportunity to create a new product for an established market. They came up with a creative idea to use RFID technology to collect new and more detailed data than had ever been collected before in the tradeshow industry. They were introducing a new way to collect and disseminate information between tradeshow buyers and sellers.

The technology was new, but the problem was not. Their competitors had already conditioned the market by providing a lower-technology solution. It was too costly for the competitor to convert to RFID and their technology only enabled them to capture a limited set of information. The media company's offering provided more detailed data, delivered in a creative way using a new and innovative technology. They didn't have to create a new market; they leveraged an existing one.

Customers that have a competitive product have a defined need that you can address. Leverage the fact that your competitors may have already conditioned your target market to the problem, you only need to find a more innovative solution to the same problem. Experienced customers know what they like and what they don't. They just need a reason to switch. They will see greater value in a product that changes their current experience for the better.

The impulse to imitate a competitor keeps you one step behind the leader.

Does your organization find it easier to imitate a competitor?

Are there more innovative ways to solve existing problems in the market?

8.5 Blank Page

Sometimes starting with a blank page makes more sense than trying to envision the next iteration of a product. Product line extensions are important, but it is increasingly difficult to stay ahead of the competition. Trying to enhance an existing product may extend the product lifecycle for a while, but not for long. It may be easier to create a new market or find a niche opportunity and exploit it than to compete head-on. *Don't be afraid to create a new market.*

Creating a new market requires a greater leap of faith than developing new product line extensions. It requires a greater level of creativity and risk, yet it can be far more rewarding in terms of revenue and profitability. Make sure you have the right mechanisms in place to validate and evaluate these opportunities. There must be a strong business case to justify taking this risk.

A major regional bank developed a strategy and program to create a new market. They wanted to develop a specific program for women to increase the banks opportunity to do more business with them. The idea was just an idea when the entrepreneurial leader was hired to develop and run with it. The leader had spent many years in banking, but also had experience as an entrepreneur and as a consultant. Up to this point the bank had limited experience with new business ventures. There had been plenty of new business ideas, but not much sustainable success.

The bank understood the importance of conducting extensive research to ensure that the business idea was viable and in lock step with the direction of the bank. Once the business opportunity was confirmed, the leader put together a small group to get started. The leader was fortunate to have a strong commitment from the top and a clear strategy to follow. Another key ingredient was ownership, having a leader who lived and breathed the business everyday. All the pieces were in place; leadership, strategy, resources and ownership.

The business required a lot of relationship-building, both internally and externally, to get going. The team encountered a number of obstacles and barriers along the way. They leveraged those processes that supported their efforts and worked around those that did not. Although the process was not always smooth, the new business was eventually launched successfully across six states, thanks to the commitment and dedication of the entrepreneurial leader and the team.

In two years, the business had gained national attention and was envied by some of the largest banks in the industry. Eight years later, the business was still going strong. The bank found that starting with a blank page helped them build a successful new business and gain a competitive lead in the market. Perhaps the greatest achievement for the bank was success—learning how to be successful was as important as the success itself.

Even if starting with a blank page sounds a little too scary for you and your firm, try it and see what you come up with. These don't have to be major investments to be new and different, they just have to demonstrate a higher level of creativity and ingenuity than your competitors. Starting with a blank page can help people get more creative and think outside the box.

As your innovation skills increase, you will find starting with a blank page to be more exciting and challenging. The corporate entrepreneur is looking for these types of opportunities.

How often do you start with a blank page when looking for new innovations?

8.6 Balancing Act

Risk and innovation go hand in hand. There are all types of risk when you are getting started in creating a culture of innovation. Financial risk is the one that you think of first, but there are other risks: technical, market, and organizational. These risks are normally factored into the evaluation process. Other risks include not making experimentation part of the innovation process and not leveraging what you've learned from your successes and failures. Another is the risk of losing the most entrepreneurial people you have. Far too little time is spent understanding these risks in terms of their impact on the organization. *There is a need to find the right balance of risk and innovation.*

Financial risk is inherent in all innovations. Managing financial risk can be effective if key aspects of risk management are in place and individuals are trained in it. Establishing a set of risk measurements for new innovations provides a financial filter for new ideas. Developing policies and procedures helps encourage and support risk-taking. Embedding risk management into the culture helps individuals take responsibility for managing risk.

Technical, market and organizational risks are an integral part of the development of innovations. Like financial risks, they must be identified and managed. Technical risks refer to whatever can cause major disruptions in the development process: issues with developing a new technology or application, a major disruption in manufacturing the product, or the introduction of a new technology by a competitor. These risks must be factored into the development process.

Marketing risks relate to the need, adoption and acceptance of your product in the market. Initial beta tests can seem promising, but the product can fail once it comes to market. Estimating the size of the market or forecasting sales can create market risk, as can not taking the time to evaluate product concepts. One firm spent extensive time and resources testing new product concepts in the market. They would often do thirty or more iterations of a product idea before settling on the final product.

Organizational risks are often related to a shift in ownership or sponsorship of a project. Perhaps the project leader moves on to another position in the company or the project is no longer in alignment with the organization's strategic objectives. The sponsor may be transferred or take on new responsibilities. A key technical resource could be recruited to another project. Any one of these risks can kill the prospects for your product or business.

The level of risk is different for incremental versus radical innovations. Radical innovations carry with them substantial risks. Jumping into radical innovation without the proper mindset and infrastructure can be disastrous. Incremental innovations are less risky, but they do not go far enough in making the necessary organizational changes that will be required to embrace radical innovations. Incremental innovations do, however, provide a launching pad for innovation. Once you have established a track record of successful incremental innovations, it is easier and less risky to create radical innovations. Finding the right mix will help you manage risks.

It is here, as well, where experimentation helps in building your organization's capability to manage risk. Experimentation enables you to minimize risks up front and develop a higher degree of comfort in taking risks. As you move to a culture of innovation, your confidence in taking and managing risks increases. Funding only a few innovations a year might make sense financially, but does little to build the organizational competency required to embed innovation into the culture.

Experimentation and failure go hand in hand. Failure is part of the learning process. It is also something that many organizations have been reluctant to adopt. The mantra in many organizations is that "failure is not an option" which leaves little room for experimentation. The problem is that playing it safe is no longer an option.

You will also want to capture the lessons you learn from both success and failure. Leveraging that knowledge moving forward can save you time and money. Many organizations fail to take this into consideration. Failures are inevitable; it is how you handle them that will make the difference. If failure is treated as part of the learning process, then there is greater receptivity to innovation. If failure is seen as career-limiting then people will be more reluctant to be involved in it. There is risk either way.

A greater risk is losing some of your most talented employees: your corporate entrepreneurs. They are not likely to stick around if there is not a concerted effort to promote innovation and entrepreneurial activity in the organization. They are easily bored, will get frustrated, and most likely leave. These individuals are the ones willing to take the calculated risks, bend rules, and do whatever it takes to make new innovations successful. Losing them could be a great risk to your efforts to build a culture of innovation.

One entrepreneurial leader said that he is happier doing what he does as an employee, but organizations don't know what to do with him once a project is completed. He doesn't seem to fit the corporate mold, and finding a traditional role for him in the organization does not make sense from his perspective. Even though he would prefer to stay, he feels he has no choice but to leave the company. This is a common complaint among corporate entrepreneurs. Despite the investment organizations have made in these senior executives, they are willing to let them walk out the door. They are walking out with the knowledge and expertise they need to become more innovative—at another company.

Balancing risk and innovation is multi-dimensional. It must be identified, managed, and mitigated if you intend to establish innovation as a core competency.

Are you doing a good job of balancing risk and innovation?

_____

What types of risk is your organization ignoring?

_____

8.7 Value Creation

Innovations can be internal or external to the organization. Although much of the focus on innovation is on external innovation, there is plenty of room for innovation inside organizations. Both types of innovation provide viable opportunities for creating value. Internal innovations used to enhance and transform internal systems and processes can create value for customers downstream. Process, marketing and organizational innovations can contribute to enhanced customer experiences. External innovations create value for your customers and can become an integral part of your customer's solution for their own clients. *Both internal and external innovations create value.*

A new internal process can be just as important as a new technology. Like incremental and radical innovation, internal and external forms of innovation provide different venues for developing innovation as a core competency. They also create different opportunities to create value. Look for innovation opportunities in both.

Internal innovations can be useful in establishing a foothold for innovation in an organization. New process innovations can improve development, production and delivery of products and services to customers. Marketing innovations can help organizations get closer to customer needs. Organizational innovations can create new environments that encourage innovative behavior. These types of innovation help get more people involved in the innovation process and can often translate into value for customers.

Funding for the best ideas can accelerate learning and provide an opportunity for experimentation. Internal innovations require the same types of due diligence and evaluation. They require the same level of discipline to be done effectively. Teams find that they must become adept at managing budgets and dealing with risk. The value that is created is visible and measurable. Innovation has both personal and business value when it is created this way.

External innovations are more complex and require a deeper level of understanding about value creation. Identifying key stakeholders and understanding what value creation means for them will help you build that value into the innovation. Value creation must be customer-oriented. One of the largest reasons for product failures is the lack of a clear understanding of customer and market needs. Many innovations look great on paper but fall flat in the market. Too often, new innovations lose sight of the real value they offer to the end customer. They neglect to factor in usability, purpose, meaning, experience or real need.

The term "next bench syndrome" was most frequently used in the high-tech industry. It referred to engineers who were sitting next to each other and coming up with great product ideas among themselves without the insight or input of the organization's customers. The result was a proliferation of really cool products that didn't go anywhere in the market. Surely those days are gone—or are they?

Customers must be an integral part of the value creation process. They provide valuable input into new product and service ideas. Traditional approaches to market research may not be adequate. More companies are digging deeper and getting customers actively involved in new product development. Organizations are using ethnography to get a better handle on the beliefs, values, desires and behaviors of customers. Ethnography refers to the study of culture and people's lives. Organizations that are using ethnography are uncovering new product opportunities. The traditional approach of starting with technology and ending with customers has been reversed.

No matter whether you are focused on internal or external innovations the key is to be sure they create value. Value for the customer translates into value for the organization.

Do you focus on internal or external innovations?

_____

How do you go about getting customer input into value creation?

_____

8.8 Measures and Metrics

Many organizations see innovation as the answer to business growth. A recent study suggested that more than 60% of companies have innovation as a strategic priority. Yet despite the hype, innovation has not delivered on its promise. As discussed earlier, innovation alone is not the answer. Building an organization that can sustain innovation over time is what is important. Defining value drivers that support growth is what matters. The problem has been that there have been no standard measures or metrics for innovation. Executives have had no way of evaluating their company's innovation efforts. *Traditional value drivers are not enough.*

Traditional value drivers are good for business as usual, but they do little to support, encourage or promote innovation. It is increasingly difficult to manage innovation projects when you have no measures or metrics to help you determine the value of innovation. Even the United States government—which tracks investments in software, equipment, and buildings—does not track intangible investments in innovation: brand equity, training and development of talent, and new product design—all of which are estimated to be in the billions of dollars. This misses some of the fastest-growing parts of the GDP.

A lack of innovation measures and metrics puts an innovation project at a distinct disadvantage. Entrepreneurial leaders have found that traditional value drivers can be an impediment to moving their projects forward and getting the required funding. Many are forced to adhere to traditional metrics, but develop new ones that align with the goals of the project itself. As in an entrepreneurial startup, the uncertainty that is inherent in new innovations is only evident in hindsight.

Organizations that look at investments in innovation over various time horizons are better able to allocate funding and resources against competing projects. It levels the playing field. An organization should develop its own set of innovation metrics. Do not over—engineer them; keep them simple. Not all of your innovation metrics are financial; they should include having the right people and processes in place. Organizational and culture metrics are just as important. Focus on outcomes and determine what metrics are needed to get you there.

There are a number of innovation measures and metrics you may want to consider including some of the following:

- Innovative Ideas—number of new ideas generated

- Number of Entrepreneurial Role Models—investment in developing leaders

- Employees involved in innovation projects—percentage of employees

- Turnover—retention of corporate entrepreneurs

- Process Pipeline Flow—products in pipeline at various stages of development

- R& D Innovation Ratio—radical versus incremental innovations

- Innovation Portfolio Mix—new to company, new to world, new technology

- Sales of New Products—percent of innovation ideas successfully commercialized

- Time to Market—improved time to market

- New Product Launch—number and frequency of new product launches

- New Revenues and Profits—cumulative new product revenues and profits

- Innovation Revenue—per employee

- Impact on Growth—new product revenues versus total company revenues

- Return on Innovation Investments—shareholder value to cost of capital

- New product success rate

- New product survival rate

- R&D Spending—annual increase in R&D spending

- Intangibility Index—the ratio of R&D to capital spending times 100

The old adage is true: you get what you measure. Develop measures and metrics for innovation that encourage, motivate and drive business growth.

What measures and metrics is your organization using to drive business growth?

SUMMARY: Chapter 8: Lead the Way with Experimentation— *Innovation*

Innovation is the second building block of corporate entrepreneurship. Many organizations view it as the answer to their growth problem. The roots of innovation were grounded in technology, but extend beyond technology. Innovation also refers to the integration of new ideas into products and services. Many organizations lack an understanding of the interrelationship between corporate entrepreneurship and innovation. Corporate entrepreneurship provides the infrastructure to support innovation, whether incremental or radical. The most successful innovative companies have created the entrepreneurial mindset and infrastructure to support innovation.

Organizations focused on developing innovation as a core competency find that keeping innovations linked to the core business is less risky. Doing so enables the organization to leverage existing resources and expertise. Incremental innovations make it easier to build confidence and the skills required to tackle more radical innovations. Experimenting with both helps the organization build an innovation process that fits their culture and risk profile. Until you start experimenting, you will not understand which systems, processes, and practices get in the way and which ones support innovation.

Compromising creativity out of an idea is easy when you try to eliminate risk or incorporate everyone's ideas into a product or service. Settling on the lowest common denominator can take the uniqueness out of the idea and lower its market value. Ensure that you keep creativity in your innovations. Starting with a blank page can often be easier than trying to imitate a competitor. Creating a new market requires a keen sense for identifying and exploiting niche opportunities. You can also leverage the goodwill and marketing that your competitors have created in the market to launch a new product.

There is risk inherent in all innovations. Finding the right balance of innovation and risk will take time. Looking at risk from all sides—financial, technical, market, and organizational—will ensure that you've covered all the bases. Leveraging both internal and external innovations can create value for you and your customers. Identify internal and external ways to create value. Establishing innovation measures and metrics will enable you to better evaluate your innovation efforts.

Innovation is a competency that can be achieved if the organization is willing to change.

Corporate Entrepreneur Insights and Lessons Learned

- Innovation—"Innovation is all about creating things from thin air."

- Challenging—"Doing it outside the mother ship or germinating from within are equally challenging."

- Spirit of Innovation—"The spirit of innovation is a reflection of the environment that you work in. We set up shop in an abandoned warehouse, painted the walls chartreuse, set up a coffee bar and had telephone booths in the corner to set the stage for creativity and innovation."

- Innovation—"There are lots of ideas; the challenge is making the right choice. That is what is so difficult. We developed a rigorous evaluation process that enabled us to separate the good ideas from the not-so-good."

- Strong Market Research—"Finding unmet customer needs requires rigorous market research. Testing 30 to 50 versions of a product is not unusual in our industry."

- Market Need—"The months of primary research solidified the market need and the financial model showed profitability within 18 to 24 months. As an information services business, we had the benefit of leveraging existing knowledge and expertise that had significant brand equity."

- Usability Testing—"Usability testing put the customer in front of our product development efforts."

- Customer Input—"We used video clips of customers using the beta products to convince senior management to get the funding we needed."

- Value Chain—"Our customers were all in the information business, so our service was designed to be an integral part of our customers' value chain."

- Complexity—"There is a lot of complexity in developing a global product. Products are marginalized down to the lowest common denominator, which decreases its value to each market."

- New Knowledge—"More importantly, our service provided something unique; we were creating new knowledge and insights for our customers."

- Balance—"You need to find a balance between experimentation and pragmatism."

Chapter 9

Adaptability Opens the Door

Change

9.1   Change to Grow—embedding *change* in the organization to grow

9.2   Fear—*fear* of the known and unknown gets in the way

9.3   Unfreezing—getting through the *change process* is tough

9.4   Fitting In—being *adaptable* is the key that opens the door to change

9.5   Finding Yourself—you will need to hold a *mirror* up to yourself and the organization

9.6   Your Mission—like it or not, you are now the *change agents* of the company

9.7   On Stage—be prepared to be in the *spotlight*, success and failure have a price

Corporate Entrepreneur Insights and Lessons Learned

9.1 Change to Grow

More than ever, organizations are under pressure to create new business growth. This need to grow requires the ability and readiness to embrace change. Corporate entrepreneurship provides the platform for that change. Traditional approaches to management no longer apply to new growth businesses. This is forcing organizations to go through an internal transformation or change process. As the external rules of the game have changed, so must the internal rules for operating a company. Change is a dynamic and ongoing process. *Embedding change in the organization leads to growth.*

Change is one of the most misunderstand and underdeveloped skills in organizations. It is multi-dimensional and touches every aspect of the organization. It deals with the soft skills. It requires an understanding of human systems. It requires a shift in thinking and behavior. It changes the balance of power and politics. It is a process and an outcome. The process is designed to facilitate the change, and the outcome is the results you hope to achieve from the change.

An organization's readiness and willingness to change are key determinants of how quickly change happens. The willingness to change is dependent on the organization's stated goal to change and what is expected from that change. The need to change must be clearly articulated. The CEO must set the tone for the change. The readiness to change is dependent on the ability to change current organizational systems, policies, and procedures. It is also dependent on the readiness of individuals to accept and embrace change as part of the growth process. Both the desire for and belief in change must be there for it to gain support.

Change itself is situational. Even if only the entrepreneurial team is going through the change process, the core business will need to accept and acknowledge the change. The process will change the team and individuals that participated. The rest of the organization will have to accept the change for the value it brings to the organization, even if they are not directly involved in the change.

The challenge with change is the unlearning and relearning that must occur for change to happen. This includes unlearning attitudes, beliefs, and values that are part of the very fabric of the organization. It requires building new attitudes, beliefs, and values that support the new entrepreneurial culture. Change occurs at the individual, team, and organizational levels so it ripples throughout the organization.

The change will create a new culture that must now co-exist with the core culture. These dual cultures will by nature be in conflict with one another. Often there is a sharp contrast between the new culture and the old. A new reality has emerged from the collective learning and shared experience of the team. They have created new values, operating processes, rules of engagement, behaviors, and norms. They have created a new personality that sets them apart from the old culture. This causes internal tension and conflict, especially when both cultures must work together.

Change requires an understanding of the complexities and intricacies of creating an environment where both the core business and growth initiatives can co-exist. Both cultures are needed to build and sustain growth over time. The entrepreneurial team will find themselves standing outside looking in. The rest of the organization will wonder what the new culture is all about.

Change is a powerful force that changes the dynamics of an organization. An organization needs to change if it wants to grow.

Does your organization have the ability, willingness, and readiness for change?

9.2 Fear

Change is frightening because it forces you to trust in something that you cannot see. There are two types of fear, fear of the unknown and fear of the known. Fear of the unknown is the field of possibilities. It represents an opportunity to create something that may have never existed before or to develop a major breakthrough on an existing problem. This type of fear is grounded in not knowing. Fear of the known is something that people face as well. Knowing that something didn't work in the past becomes the justification for your resistance to trying something similar again. Past experiences cloud your thinking. This type of fear is grounded in knowing. *Both fear of the known and unknown get in the way.*

Fear is a creation of your own imagination. It stems from an inherent distrust in something or someone. It is a paralyzing force that prevents you from acting or doing something that you believe will cause harm. It is easy to associate something with fear of the known because of an experience you may have had that was harmful or dangerous. Your fear is often grounded in those experiences and there is a natural tendency to tread lightly when it comes to doing anything similar. Such fear can stop you in your tracks. It prevents you from experimenting, testing the water, and figuring things out. It stops you from thinking about options.

Fear of the unknown is just as debilitating. It is something that you create in your own mind based on a gut feeling, intuition, or belief. You may not have the data to support your fear, but it seems real enough to stop you. Change requires an exploration of the unknown. You don't know what you don't know until you see it. It doesn't matter whether it is a change in behavior, a new way of working, or developing an innovative product. Fear gets in the way and slows the change process.

Can you imagine all the modern advances of the twentieth century that would not exist today if fear of the unknown had stopped those inventors from pushing forward? Only when you step inside the unknown will you truly understand what is possible. The fear of the unknown is what excites and motivates corporate entrepreneur. They are creating something that they cannot see but only envision, and they enjoy exploring the unknown.

Fear

Known	Unknown
Experience	Possibilities

The fear of change has both internal and external roots. Change is usually motivated by an external force. This external force can come from outside or within the company. Change is also an internal psychological process that people go through. Each individual has their own fears and limits on what they believe is possible. Individuals who have worked in environments of change are more likely to face the fear that the change brings. Individuals who have worked in traditional organizations may let fear influence their thinking and behavior.

Fear is viewed through a personal and professional lens. Executives in particular may prefer to stick with the facts and what they know from past experience. Entrepreneurial leaders, on the other hand, are often avid learners and exploring the unknown is an adventure for them. Team members may have the greatest fears given their status and position in the organization.

Finding out what level of fear exists within yourself and your team will be important in setting the parameters for how quickly you will be able to change.

Does fear get in your way?

9.3 Unfreezing

Organizational change experts say that in order to change you must go through three phases: unfreeze, change, and refreeze. Unfreezing is breaking away from the way you operate today. Change is the actual process you go through to transform yourself. Refreezing refers to the ability to form new ways of operating. Over time, you become hardened to the reality of the business culture you are working in. You embrace the organization's processes and align your behaviors accordingly. Stepping outside those boundaries often has consequences. Corporate entrepreneurs are expected to do just that, step outside of the traditional behaviors they have been conditioned to adhere to. *Getting through the change process is tough.*

The ability to change is different from the willingness to change. Most corporate entrepreneurs embrace the opportunity to change. Yet it is their inability to change that gets in the way. They fall back on what is known, comfortable, and acceptable. Although each individual has a capacity to change, it may require some coaching and reinforcement to make the change.

The fundamental problem for corporate entrepreneurs is that they do not know what they are expected to change into. In many cases they are creating the change as they move through the process of seeing what works, discarding what doesn't, and testing new approaches that may streamline current procedures. It takes time to create and formulate a new set of operating principles that will work effectively. There are challenges of balancing the old with the new and gaining acceptance along the way. A process that might work well for the team may often be unacceptable to the rest of the organization.

Change Process

There is an inherent anxiety in being asked to change. Change is uncomfortable. There is uncertainty and risk associated with changing. Corporate entrepreneurs must be willing to live with uncertainty and deal with different levels of risk. There is also the anxiety of learning something new. Learning is a key attribute of corporate entrepreneurs; they love to learn new things. Then there is incorporating the change into your behavior. Once the team has made the transition, the change will be evident in their behavior.

Understanding where you are today and where you want to be is helpful. Conducting a culture assessment is a valuable way to look at the current environment and compare it to one that is more entrepreneurial. Visually showing the data will help everyone understand the magnitude of the required change. Get a snapshot of what processes you may have to bend along the way. Determine the organization's readiness and willingness to change. A culture assessment can provide you with these insights.

Behavioral assessment tools will give you some understanding of an individual's response to change. Intrapreneurs score high on response to change. There are a number of assessment tools that will help you identify these individuals. These people are the ones who will be the first to unfreeze and the quickest to refreeze into a new mode of operation.

Find these individuals and let them take the lead. Their example will set a standard for the rest of the team.

How would you rate your organization's willingness and ability to change?

_____

Who are the individuals with a high propensity to change?

_____

9. 4 Fitting In

Corporate entrepreneuring is not for everyone. The experience is often grueling and extremely stressful, but the experience itself is what brings the greatest joy. You will need to adapt and cope with uncertainty. You will be dealing with situations that you have never encountered before. There will be new challenges. You will have to make decisions with limited data and be willing to be held accountable for your actions. The corporate entrepreneur thrives in this type of environment. *Being adaptable is the key that opens the door to change*

Each experience has both positive and negative consequences. If you are not ready or able to adjust to the high pressure and uncertainty, then the experience can have very negative effects. These often play out in the workplace or at home. Long hours and twelve-hour days are enough to drive anyone a little crazy. Tensions rise and so do tempers. The stress and strain will be visible to your family. It will take an emotional and physical toll on you. They will wonder if it is all worth it. You will spend time convincing them that it is.

One corporate entrepreneur had season tickets to the symphony orchestra. So as not to disappoint her husband, she would drag herself away from work and literally fall into her chair in the concert hall. It took every ounce of energy for her to stay awake. It didn't take long for her to be fast asleep. At least the concert gave her an opportunity to take a well-deserved break, maybe even clear her head. However, the concert would have been much more enjoyable if she had had the energy to enjoy it.

These experiences test your ability to adapt and your flexibility to work under pressure. It is a physically taxing experience that requires great energy and stamina, both of which can quickly become depleted if not kept in balance. You will need a high level of energy to manage the pressure, and adaptability to deal with the uncertainty. Being adaptable makes it easier to accept change, while vitality gives you the energy to deal with it.

You want individuals on the team who are highly adaptable, work well under pressure, and have a high tolerance for ambiguity. You've heard the phrase "strong as the weakest link." This is often the case with new initiatives. If a few individuals are slow to adapt and change, it holds the rest of the team back. One team struggled with taking the time to bring everyone up to speed or leave some members behind. Some individuals were having trouble coping and keeping up with the change. The rest of the team decided that they could not wait and pushed forward.

You must constantly evaluate how you are doing. Your energy level will be a good barometer for how well you are holding up. Everyone will get exhausted. It is part of the process, but individuals who manage their own well-being are better able to cope with unexpected surprises. You need to be emotionally and physically prepared to handle change.

Find a way to balance the stress of work and your commitments at home. Keep track of your energy, your stress, and your ability to cope.

How adaptable are you?

_____

Do you have a lot of energy and stamina?

_____

9.5 Finding Yourself

The role of a corporate entrepreneur is not easy. There is no guidebook to help you along the way. Part of the excitement of being a corporate entrepreneur is exploring the breadth and depth of your own skills and abilities. The experience will test the very limits of your abilities and challenge your thinking. It will shake the very foundation of your beliefs and philosophies about work, and it will enable you to see the core business in a different light. Many of these experiences will be unsettling, but others will be exhilarating. It forces you to *hold a mirror up to yourself* and the organization.

Corporate entrepreneurs will welcome the opportunity to flex their muscle and test their abilities. They want the opportunity to use skills and capabilities that are underutilized. They know intuitively that they can do more, but they may not have had an opportunity to demonstrate it. They use these types of initiatives as a way to get the experience that may be missing from their personal portfolio of skills. Working in an entrepreneurial environment gives them the room to explore and enhance those capabilities. It helps them accelerate their personal growth.

You begin to realize that you are in control of your own growth and development. You are energized with the knowledge that you are free to explore your own abilities and stretch yourself beyond what you thought was possible. How far you decide to push outside your comfort zone is your choice. How far the team drags you outside your comfort zone is another. Either way, you will have changed.

The mirror will be a reflection of where you are at any point in time. It will be motivating and encouraging, and you will take pride in what you've accomplished. You will be surprised at how easy some things are and how difficult others can be. As you move forward you will increase your self-worth and confidence. You will be encouraged to step up to the table and take on more challenges. In turn, you must be willing to accept the negative consequences of what you see. The key is how you deal with what you learn from the experience.

The mirror will also be held up to the organization. You will see the organization for what it is and what it needs to become to transition to a more entrepreneurial culture. It may be more difficult for the organization to see what it has become and accept how far it has to go. It is often threatening and challenging. Holding the mirror up is a double-edged sword. The organization will have to find ways to deal with the things that must change. You will have a clearer picture of what needs to change in order to help the organization make that transition. You will also see the very change you are trying to achieve in the mirror. The mirror is not forgiving. Take a look often.

You will have to take ownership for what you see. The organization will have to take ownership for what it sees.

What is it you see when you look in the mirror?

_____

What do you think the organization will see?

_____

9.6 Your Mission

Your mission is to be the change agent for the organization. A change agent is tasked with helping the organization transition to a new way of operating, in this case becoming more entrepreneurial. Change is the most difficult part of the process and it will be a major issue that gets in the way. While the thought of change is exciting, actually implementing the change is much harder, especially when everyone around you is quite happy remaining in the comfort of the existing culture. *Like it or not, you are now the change agent for the company.*

The new initiative is often seen as way to facilitate the change process and pave the way for future change. Unless you are undertaking a major organizational transformation, there is usually no formal change program associated with smaller projects. That creates higher hurdles for the entrepreneurial team. The team is usually left on its own to make the change happen. It is helpful if the change is publicly sanctioned.

As such it is often viewed as an experiment. That's why it is important that you identify those individuals who thrive in an environment of change. They will be the ones who push the edge of the envelope and seek new and innovative ways to deal with problems. It is critical to strike the right balance by having a mix of people who like change and some who are more cautious. You can actually determine how an individual will respond to change by using behavioral assessment tools that give you a quick snapshot. You can easily identify change agents.

Change for the sake of change is not good. Some change agents will want to change everything, all the time, because they continually envision new approaches. Actively managing the change process will be important. One entrepreneurial leader dealt with proliferation of new ideas this way. She got people to write down their ideas in a one-page document that explained why their idea was better than the current way. Half of the time, people would conclude on their own that the idea didn't make sense, the other half of the time they made a significant case for implementing the change. Either way, it helped the leader manage the limitless ideas that surfaced during the project.

Being a change agent is a key skill that leaders must have. If the change process is too slow or too fast, it can leave some team members frustrated and less effective. You are creating the change as you move forward. At the same time, it is a skill that all of the team members will need. Being able to deal effectively with change and accept it as part of the process will help everyone.

There are formal training programs designed specifically for change agents. It helps individuals understand the human dynamics behind change and the resistance to it. They will be better prepared to handle difficult situations and gain insights into techniques for facilitating change.

Are you willing to take on the mission of change agent in your organization?

_____

Does your organization provide training for change agents?

_____

9.7 On Stage

As the change agents for the company, you will be creating the change on stage, in front of everyone. The spotlight is great when things are going well, but can be unnerving when things aren't going so well. The fact is the company has invested in you and your team to deliver the next best thing, so being visible is part of the job. As if you were in a play, the eyes of the organization are on you. Each person has a critical part to play and there is a high expectation that together you will be successful. *Be prepared to be in the spotlight, success and failure have a price.*

The organization has committed the resources and recruited you along with others to charge ahead. Once you get started, you may find that you will not be getting all the resources you need to get the job done. In some cases it is not always clear what you needed in the first place, in others it may be all that is available. Suddenly, you realize that you can't get there from here. You need to think on your feet and find new ways to address issues without always extending your hand back to the core business. They expect you to figure things out. They are looking to see if you can.

The need to change is no more apparent than when you are faced with challenges you've never dealt with before. The fact is that you will face a number of these challenges and this is part of the learning experience. You will encounter situations that the core business has not had to deal with before. They will be looking for you to deal with them. You may have to find alternative resources to solve specific problems, or you may need to change course to avoid creating bigger issues down the road. Either way the spotlight is on you.

Being on stage is most difficult when things are not going so well, especially when you hit a wall. Nerves are frayed and tension is high among team members. The long hours and doubts that creep into the group during this period will be visible to all, no matter how well you think it is contained within the group. This is also a time when others in the organization who have less sympathy will prey on those harboring doubts. There will always be those inside the organization, for whatever reason, who may not want your initiative to be successful. Accept this and don't let it take you further off track. The organization will be looking to see how you deal with these situations.

The positive side of being on stage is that you get an opportunity to demonstrate your value and contribution to the organization. You've stepped up to the challenge and have signed up for the risk. There are many in the organization who are not willing to put their job or career on the line. You know that win or lose, you have grabbed the opportunity to grow and experience something that has increased your own personal and professional value. You are charting your own destiny.

All of this is visible and open to public scrutiny. As you encounter and resolve these situations, you are laying the groundwork for future projects. There will be many detours along the way.

Being in the spotlight has its pros and cons. There are no rehearsals. You deal with things as they happen and incorporate what you learned into changing the way things are done. You are paving the way for change.

Are you prepared to be in the spotlight?

SUMMARY: Chapter 9: Adaptability Opens the Door—*Change*

Change is the third building block of corporate entrepreneurship. Change is one of the most difficult and underdeveloped skills in organizations. The ability to develop innovation as a core competency requires embracing change and making it an explicit organizational objective. Change starts at the top with a commitment from the CEO. It is not always the willingness to change but the ability to change that gets in the way. The ability to change is a learning process that individuals and organizations must go through. The readiness to change will be contingent on the organization's willingness to change current systems, policies, and procedures to support innovation.

Embedding change in the organization is the best way for organizations to grow. Change itself is situational and does not occur spontaneously. It is both an internal and external process. Change is usually motivated by an external factor, but is dealt with as an internal psychological process by individuals. External factors can be used to facilitate the change, but internally you must be prepared to deal with the change. The resistance to change is often grounded in fear, whether fear of the known or fear of the unknown. Both can stop individuals and organizations from exploring beyond what is currently known.

Change requires a three-step approach: unfreeze, change, and refreeze. First, you must let go of the existing systems. Second, you must change the way you do things. Third, you must adopt the new way of operating. Change is uncomfortable and creates a certain level of anxiety. Individuals can feel threatened by changes in the organization's political climate and shifts in the balance of power. Change is both frightening and enlightening for those who thrive in an environment of change.

Being adaptable is a key behavior that is required for change. Inflexible individuals find it difficult to accept change. Change also requires taking a hard look at yourself and the organization. Holding a mirror up to the organization can be unsettling. Corporate entrepreneurs are the change agents for the organization, so there is an expectation that you will lead the change. In reality, you will be creating the change as you move forward. Be prepared to be in the spotlight. Everything you do will be visible. Use the spotlight to demonstrate your value and what you are capable of doing.

Change is required to propel the organization forward to achieve its innovation goals.

Corporate Entrepreneur Insights and Lessons Learned

- Transition—"The business reality was that the company needed to transition to a new operating model and new technology to stay competitive."

- Change Agent—"You need someone to set the stage for change, someone known to be a change agent who can lead the change."

- Force Change—"Sometimes you have to force change. Many people are happy with the status quo. They will not change unless they are forced to change."

- Self-Realization—"These types of initiatives force you to see what you are made of, your strengths and weaknesses."

- Ability to Change—"The need to change was a necessity but the inability of the organization to change was the big bottleneck. Change like this was threatening the very foundation of the organization, and the perceived shift in power was downright nerve-racking for some."

- Willingness to Change—"Prior to taking on this task, I had told the executive sponsor that we would probably have to break rules and step on toes to make this happen. At the time he seemed to understand and acknowledge it as part of the change process. Accepting this behavior when it actually happened would be a test of his willingness to change."

- Loyalty—"It is loyalty to the cause that becomes the cornerstone for most change initiatives."

- Life of Change Agent—"Despite my attempts to ensure that all of the factors were in place for success (funding, management support, adequate resources, executive sponsor, and so on), life for me as the change agent was fraught with land mines. Some things I was waiting for, others caught me by surprise."

- Not Invented Here—"We found that jealousy and resistance got in the way of integrating new business/products/services back into the organization."

- Creating Change—"They were intelligent, trusting, creative, open, honest, and stubborn. And they created rituals and new ways of working that remained an enigma to the rest of the organization."

Chapter 10

Hit the Target with Precision

Execution

10.1 Building Boats

E xecuting with precision takes time. Building execution as a core competency takes practice. Think of it as a complex set of interrelated variables that must come together perfectly to achieve precision. Precision in execution begins with a clear understanding of the end goal and the intended business benefits. It requires clarity of vision, a process to get there, and the ability to deliver business value. It also requires having the right skills and expertise. Execution is a core competency of corporate entrepreneurs. *It involves more than building a boat that floats.*

Execution is not an event but an integral part of the development process. It is an attitude, a competence, and a set of behaviors that motivate people to bring things to closure. If you want to develop execution as a core competency, you must build the infrastructure and skills to support it. It starts with integrating execution hurdles into project plans at stage gates and major milestones. It requires leveraging those individuals who have the skills and behaviors to effectively execute. It means acknowledging, recognizing, and rewarding individuals for execution. It requires a clear understanding that execution is not just about getting it done but getting it done right.

At some point in your career you may have participated in one of those team-building experiences like Outward Bound. In one exercise, they give you the parts to build something without any instructions. You've got a minimum amount of time to plan, develop, and deliver. In one instance, a group of individuals working on a new business was on an off-site retreat for some team-building. The team was broken up into two smaller teams and each team was told to build a boat from a pile of robes, pieces of wood, steel drums, etc., and then take it out to the middle of a lake. Given that it was fall and the lake water was very cold, there was a high interest in seeing that it got done right.

Everyone was asked to participate, everyone was asked to contribute, and everyone was asked to leverage their expertise. Fortunately, one person on the first team had been a Boy Scout and knew how to tie nautical knots. Another had been around boats most of his life. Another understood the importance of balance and so on. Execution is all about getting everyone focused on the same goal, leveraging everyone's expertise, and getting them to work effectively together.

Hierarchy and titles don't really matter when you are focused on execution. The person with the expertise steps forward to lead the way. Not everyone will be able to contribute, but they can support the efforts of others who can. It is the experience itself that builds the behaviors you will need to develop execution as a competency. Having team members with diverse and complementary skills is essential. A team without this may suffer.

The first team, which had people with boating experience, quickly got to work building the boat. The second team, which did not have the same breadth of expertise, struggled. It was obvious that the first team had a distinct competitive advantage. Just when time began running out, the first team launched its boat with everyone on board. As the first team rowed out to the middle of the lake, the sailor on the team stood on the boat and yelled a victory cheer.

Once they were back on dry land, they all began to talk about how they would do it differently next time. They had executed well, yet they talked about ways they could build a better boat. Apparently a few of the team members almost fell out of the boat and some of the others got wet. Building the boat was one goal and making it float was another, but getting everyone out to the lake and back safely was just as important.

Execution requires getting all the pieces to come together in a coordinated and timely fashion. It takes time and practice. It requires full participation by everyone to achieve challenging goals and implement successfully. Leveraging expertise across the team will be important. Allowing those with good execution skills to lead the way can help ensure that things get done. Developing execution as a core competency can make the difference in getting the project done on time, on budget, with the intended business results.

Execution is a competency that you will want to build to deliver business value.

What does your organization do to increase its ability to execute with precision?

10.2 Clarity of Vision

Clarity of vision is essential when it comes to execution. Even if you think everyone understands the end game, they do and they don't. Each individual or group has their own interpretation. The individuals who originated the idea have one perspective, the team developing it has a different perspective, and the executives who funded the project have another. Not everyone sees what they need to see, and so it is up to you as the leader to bring clarity. Clarity of vision is one end of the spectrum, execution is at the other. *Getting people on the same page is a critical aspect of execution.*

Getting to clarity is an ongoing process that requires open dialogue and discussion. There can be a million interpretations for a word depending on your point of view. The same is true of a vision. A vision that seems clear to one person will represent something different to someone else. The vision is framed around a person's mental model and what that vision means to them personally and professionally. They may see it for what they hope it will be, not for what it is in reality. Getting a common understanding of the vision will be important in laying out the roadmap for implementing it.

Unfortunately, visions take on a life of their own. As the project evolves the vision will shift, and so will the process for getting there. Not until you move forward can you begin to see what the idea really is and what it can become. The original vision can morph into something bigger and bolder. Not everyone will see that the vision has changed or has become something different than originally envisioned.

Although you may have started out with a solid plan, it will change as the vision evolves. Shifts in vision can impact your implementation plans. Vision and execution need to be consistently aligned to incorporate this change in thinking. Small changes can seem inconsequential when they occur, but the compounding effect can have a huge impact on the project. It isn't always the magnitude of the change that is important, it is the uncertainty of not knowing how a shift in vision might impact the project down the road.

Both internal and external factors can impact the vision. Financial constraints, market forces, or technology advancements can shift things enough to knock you out of alignment. The implications of these factors for the vision may be clear to you, but less so to stakeholders and the rest of the organization. As the vision shifts, you will need to keep everyone aware of these changes and reset expectations.

Clarity of vision is important in keeping everyone focused on the same end goal.

How do you ensure that everyone is on the same page?

10.3 New Directions

Changing course is all part of the process. As you move forward you will find new ways to make it better, more focused on the target market, or more financially lucrative. Every change you make costs time and money and there is precious little of that to go around. A new direction means greater opportunities and new risks. Establishing criteria up front for managing change requests will enable you to deal with them more effectively when they arise. Incorporating these into plans will be important and will impact execution. *Effectively managing changes will be the key.*

Entrepreneurs are great at coming up with new ideas. Some of their ideas will have value, others will just waste time. If the changes don't add value to the bottom line then it might be best to save them for the next phase. Each new idea or change creates a detour that you must manage effectively. You will need to decide to how to deal with these detours. Change requests are one of the biggest reasons for project delays and cost overruns because they directly impact timeline lines and costs.

Discipline is required to stick with original plans and incorporate changes that make sense. The fundamentals of the business and project plans must stay on track to preserve the integrity of the plan. Changes can create unseen problems down the road. You will not understand the real impact of these changes on your project until you are racing to meet the deadline. Determining which changes are really necessary will be easier if you establish criteria for making changes and a process for evaluating the impact of those changes on current plans.

Dealing with change requests is a key part of project control. Depending on the size and complexity of your project, you may want to use a change control process. A change control process should include procedures for submitting change requests, evaluating the changes, and determining the risks. The process should also identify who will review change requests and who will make the decisions regarding the changes. You will also want to develop a process for prioritizing changes and keeping track of change requests. Not all requests will have to be dealt with immediately, but some will. Some of the changes will have an impact on execution.

Although the technology group is normally responsible for developing a technical change process, you will want to institute one for the business. You must constantly evaluate the market opportunity for the project and aligning it more closely to market needs. The decision to incorporate changes into the product development process or to wait is a tough call. At some point you will have to decide that no more changes can be accepted. Setting a cut-off date for changes too early can be just as detrimental as making changes late in the game.

Establishing a change control process can help minimize the impact these changes will have on your ability to execute.

How do you handle change requests?

10.4 High on Closure

A key to execution is having the right skill sets and competencies to drive things to closure. As the entrepreneurial leader, you will need three types of people on your team to be successful: creators, doers, and implementers. The creator is the person with the innovative ideas. The doers are task-oriented individuals. The implementers are the individuals who bring things to closure. This is a simplistic way to view your team, but all three of these roles are important when it comes to execution.

Implementers are the individuals who make things happen. They know how to get things done or figure out how to get them done. They are goal-oriented, creative, and competitive. They have good planning and negotiating skills. They work well in high-pressure situations. They are good at taking the initiative, negotiating, and motivating others. They have the execution skills required to drive projects to completion. They don't let anything get in their way. *Implementers are high on closure.*

Doers are focused on achieving objectives. They understand the big picture and can get involved in the details when they need to. They are assertive and take responsibility for their actions. They have good communication skills and are effective in instructing others. They are not afraid to stand up to authority or challenge the status quo. They are less concerned about structure and organizational obstacles that get in the way. *Doers are task-oriented and dedicated to their work.*

Creators may be easier to spot. These are the highly creative people. They are high on learning and love change. They are always looking for ways to do things better. They are big-picture thinkers and often are able to see the gestalt. They are independent and prefer to work in less structured environments. They can get bored easily and find it difficult to stay focused on the details because they are always thinking of the next idea. *Creators develop the ideas that fuel innovation.*

Use these simple descriptions as an initial filter when you are developing your team. Take a moment to mentally separate your team into these three categories. Once you've done this, you may want to use a behavioral assessment tool to get a better understanding of individual styles and work practices. Some assessment tools enable you to evaluate execution as a competency. It is a good way to ensure that you have implementers on the team.

Execution requires having the ability and skills to establish and achieve challenging goals. It means having the behaviors that enable one to be goal oriented, good at planning and time management. Being creative and competitive while taking the initiative to bring things to closure are other behaviors that contribute to execution.

Execution requires leveraging individuals who excel at execution.

Do you have the right mix of skills on your team?

_____

Who are the creators, doers, and implementers on your team?

_____

10.5 Target Practice

The goal of execution is to hit the target. This requires more than target practice. It requires that you have the right target in sight. It is clear that the project itself will change as you integrate new ideas into it. Customers will begin to see more clearly what they really want as they see more of what you are building. New competitive offerings may impact your plans. Funding constraints and changing priorities may require changes to original plans. All of these factors will impact your ultimate target. *The key to executing with precision requires hitting the bull's eye.*

Targets will shift and change many times during the duration of a project. To minimize these shifts, you will want to test assumptions with customers frequently, get them actively involved. Experiment with new ideas and integrate the feedback back into the development process. Evaluate the tradeoffs and determine what impact they will have on time lines, funding, and business value. Look at internal and external customer factors that could impact your plans. The more interaction you have with customers, the more accurate you will be in zeroing in on the target. Each time you tweak an aspect of the project it can change the target and move the bull's eye.

New product ideas need to be tested and vetted in the markets they are intended to serve. It is not unusual for product development efforts to move ahead without rigorous market analysis or product concept testing. Initial targets are often selected without enough thought to other factors that can impact the idea. One software company decided to develop a new solution for nurses in the healthcare industry. There was a clear need for a product that would eliminate the piles of paperwork that nurses had to deal with on a daily basis. The product concept had been tested with a number of nurses, the market size defined, and the benefits articulated. Given this, the company decided to proceed.

The real issue with the product was not visible until later. The issues the company encountered were the slow adoption of technology in the industry, the lack of budgets for nursing systems, and the challenge of integrating this solution with all the other systems. The company developed the product before understanding how these other factors would impact the adoption of their product. Eventually the software company found another target for their solution. This proved to be bigger, more viable target for the company. Keep in mind that your initial target may not be your final target.

Establishing interim targets is a useful way to give everyone an opportunity to get target practice. Targets need to be threaded throughout the product development process. Targets can be established at key milestones or deliverables. Individuals should be motivated and measured on meeting interim targets. Target practice enables you to increase your execution skills. The more practice, the more adept they will be at hitting the target.

At the point when you freeze the project, you can lock in the target. Alignment is what is required to achieve precision in execution. Aligning the resources and development processes is easier when the end target is finally in sight. Execution is all about alignment. It is the alignment of the vision, resources, the development process, project changes, and customer requirements to the end goals. Hitting the target is one thing, hitting the bull's eye is what counts.

Executing with precision is the real target.

How much target practice is your organization doing?

_____

Who are the individuals who excel at execution?

_____

10.6 Benefits Matter

Execution is not something that you think about at the end of a project, but throughout the project and after you've delivered it. You can complete a project on time and on budget, but if it does not deliver the business benefits intended then it was not successful. Benefits are the business value you deliver to your customers and to the bottom line. They are also the value that is developed and delivered throughout the development process. *Delivering business value is the ultimate end game.*

Benefits are defined as the outcome to which you can assign expressions of value. An entrepreneurial initiative is developed to achieve a number of benefits. These include developing a new business, product, or service to generate new business growth, but may include others like institutionalizing project discipline, developing an entrepreneurial culture, or developing innovation as a core competency. These benefits do not happen by themselves. You will want to proactively identify and manage them throughout the process.

Benefits management provides a framework for identifying, capturing and realizing benefits throughout the product development process. Think of every step in the development process as an opportunity to deliver business value or benefits. You are looking for both internal and external value. Are you developing the product in the most cost-effective way? Are there other processes that can be used to expedite development? Are you leveraging your resources in the most efficient way? Looking at benefits from this perspective can have an impact on execution.

An information-based company that was building a new business used the opportunity to work with a new technology and create an entrepreneurial culture. On the surface, the business value was developing a new revenue stream for the company. Less well-known was the value of using this initiative to get the company up to speed with a new technology that could be leveraged in other parts of the organization. There was business value in making sure that the technology group had experience with the new technology. Leveraging the new technology created higher value for their clients, which translated into higher revenues for them.

In turn, there was a need to become more entrepreneurial, and that required putting processes in place to change the way people worked. The company recognized that to stay competitive it needed to be more innovative and needed to attract people who wanted to work in that type of environment. Creating a more entrepreneurial environment helped attract, retain, and motivate employees to be more productive. Although the organization openly acknowledged the benefits of building the business, senior management understood the business benefits that would be realized from working with a new technology and creating a new culture. Both would contribute to the execution of the new business and provide longer-term value for the organization.

Benefits management provides a framework for ensuring that investments get evaluated and deployed with a solid link to benefits. Integrating benefits management into the development process helps you understand how investments should be deployed and how all of the steps are logically linked to benefits. Each benefit that is achieved takes you to a higher level of value as the project moves forward. Proactively managing benefits can help you realize those benefits.

There is no single predetermined set of benefits, nor is there one best way to realize benefits. Benefits realization is context-specific. Benefits are sought as a way to address both problems and opportunities. Look beyond the overall business value your project is intended to deliver to the organization. Determine if there are other benefits that you would like to achieve. Decide which ones will give you the greatest return. Compare the value to the risk. Link them to the project development process and set them as goals to be tracked and measured.

Also recognize that you are taking people through a change process. Benefits management can be applied here as well. Setting the context for becoming more entrepreneurial requires more than wishful thinking.

Execution requires successfully delivering the benefits intended.

Is benefits management an integral part of your existing development process?

10.7 360-Degree View

Execution requires operating with a 360-degree view of the world. If you have been to Disney World in Orlando, you may have visited the exhibit with the 360-degree theatre. You watch in amazement as the panoramic view of the country surrounds you with sights and sounds from every direction. You don't know where to look for fear of missing something. You know that you will not capture everything. As an entrepreneurial leader, you will live in this 360-degree world every day. You will serve many masters and be a slave to the project. You will need a strong desire to succeed. *Executing with precision requires 360-degree leadership.*

It will be impossible for you to know or get involved with everything. Eventually you will stop trying. As the leader you will be pulled in every direction at the same time. You will find yourself managing up, delegating down, collaborating across, and reaching outside to keep things moving. You will need to be strategic and tactical, competitive and collaborative, emphatic and hard-nosed. You will find yourself operating at both ends of the spectrum. You will feel like you are being torn in a million directions at the same time.

Thinking that you can hold everyone and everything in check will be impossible. There aren't enough hours in the day nor is there enough bandwidth in your brain to deal with every detail. Tradeoffs will have to be made. You will have to focus on high-priority issues. Leave the detail work to those who are better able to handle it. Entrepreneurial leaders are good at delegating responsibilities and not bothering with the details.

Leading and managing requires a 360-degree perspective. Delegating down can become time-consuming, especially if you don't have the bench strength below you. You may find yourself getting actively involved to pick up the slack. Even if you have bright people on your team, they may be reluctant to stretch outside their comfort zone without a lot of pushing on your part. Managing up will become one of the more neglected things you do. There never seems to be enough time, so you sacrifice your time with your boss. Collaborating across the organization and with peers will be time-consuming and frustrating. It will be easy to neglect managing politics and dealing with peers. Reaching out to customers will be the most enjoyable and rewarding thing you do if you can find the time.

Execution requires staying focused on the end goal and letting go of traditional ways of operating. You may not have the time or energy to effectively manage the political environment, stay connected with peers, or even keep yourself visible with senior management. You will find yourself totally committed to meeting your objectives. It can cost you politically and professionally, but it may be the only way for you to hit the target.

The ups and downs of an entrepreneurial initiative can be extremely taxing on the leader and the team. Even when everyone is physically exhausted on the team, they possess an innate desire to win. It is this desire that will give them the final burst of energy that will enable them to see things through to completion. Once they can see the end in sight, they will put every ounce of energy into finishing the project. You must exhibit that same desire and determination. That may be all that is left to carry you across the finish line.

Executing with precision takes a strong leader who can effectively operate in a 360-degree world.

How effective are you at leading in a 360-degree world?

SUMMARY: Chapter 10: Hit the Target with Precision— *Execution*

Execution is a core competency necessary to effectively leverage your investments in innovation. Execution is not an event; it is attitude, competence, and set of behaviors that must be developed and threaded throughout the product development process. It means more than getting the project done on time and on budget. It requires achieving the intended business benefits, revenue targets, profit margins, or market share goals. Each stage gate or deliverable provides an opportunity to integrate execution into the development process. Developing execution as a core competency takes time and practice.

Execution begins with having a clear understanding of the end game. Clarity of vision is required to ensure that everyone is working toward the same objectives. As the project evolves, the target will change and you will have to adapt your plans accordingly. Integrating new ideas into existing plans is a critical part of refining your target. Ensuring that these changes are in alignment with the firm's strategic direction will be important. Veering too far afield can create problems down the road.

There are certain individuals who excel at execution. Identifying and leveraging their skills throughout the process will help ensure that tasks are completed and things are brought to closure. Corporate entrepreneurs who are high on closure will do what it takes to get things done. They want to do more than hit the target; they want to hit the bull's eye. Hitting the bull's eye maximizes the value you can deliver to your clients and to the organization. The ultimate goal is learning to execute with precision.

Entrepreneurial leaders need a 360-degree view of their world. It is impossible for them to stay on top of every aspect of an innovation project, and eventually they will learn to give up. There will never be enough hours in the day. The leader will be pulled in every direction and struggle to manage up, down, across, and out with clients at the same time. They will have to let things slip off their plate and make professional sacrifices. In turn, they will be energized and motivated by what they are doing. For some leaders, this will be the high point of their career.

Executing with precision will be one of your greatest achievements.

Corporate Entrepreneur Insights and Lessons Learned

- Precision—"Precision is about marrying an idea with a market opportunity."

- Pressure—"Of course you have to realize that the pressure was on us to deliver something that many thought was impossible, and many people were waiting for us to fail. They were critical of the effort and were more willing to criticize than to help."

- Marketing—"We consistently see bad marketing and branding. There is bad alignment with customer needs and what the company means to do. There is a need to innovate in marketing."

- Smoke and Mirrors—"Pre-selling a product idea when it is only smoke and mirrors can make it more difficult when you go to build it. Especially when you have no idea what it is going to take to build it."

- Handoff—"The hardest part is handing a product over to those who will launch it. It can be a difficult and costly transition. Things would break down if there was not a smooth transition from development to product launch."

- Closure—"Closure for us is often an open-ended story. We get the product developed, then hand it off to be launched. We may not be involved in it after that."

- Success—"We would have preferred to hit some singles, doubles, and triples before we had to hit a home run. Eventually we started doing product line extensions, which helped reinforce what we were doing."

- Value—"The team did not waver despite the uncertainty of future funding and potential disposition of some of the assets that were part of our business. They recognized that the real value in moving forward was the experience itself."

- Winner—"We had customers who wanted to sign up for the service even though they knew it was only partially complete. The perception of what the product could be far exceeded the reality of what the product actually was at this point. The reaction was the same in the US and abroad. We knew we had a winner."

•   Personal Joy—"Part of the joy is seeing customers get excited about the products. It was personally gratifying to roll out products that customers loved."

As a corporate entrepreneur your focus is on seeing the idea come to life. By adopting the principles of corporate entrepreneurship, you will transform yourself, your professional life and the business world that surrounds you.

THE END

Appendix

Appendix A—Corporate Entrepreneurs Core Competencies

Corporate Entrepreneur Profile™ and The Devine Group

Core Competencies	Definition
Accountability	Follows up & holds employees accountable for completion of work
Adaptability	Deals with the unexpected challenges or circumstances.
Challenge/Growth/Change	Displays willingness to take risks to change current comfort zone.
Collaborative	Establishes effective work relationships, willingly, skillfully, manages conflict
Engaged & Thriving	Driven and motivated by the excitement of a challenge
Execution	Ambition & execution skills to establish & achieve challenging goals
Independent Thinking	Prefer the freedom to create new and innovative approaches, self-reliant
Leadership Effectiveness	Integrates resources to meet objectives and ensures competitive advan
Market/Customer Focused	Initiates actions to meet market and customer needs
Motivating	Displaying ability to understand & motivates team members and then do it
Navigating Uncertainty	Ability to deal proactively with ambiguity and the unknown
Passionate Communication	Openly express thoughts and feelings, transparency
Problem Solving	Defines complex problems and brings about viable solutions.
Self Awareness	Self-knowledge of strengths & needs, can identify gaps in skill set
Strategic & Analytical Thinking	Develops broad, long-ranged objectives & plans that meet contingencies.
Takes Action	Displays resolve to follow through to honor commitments to self & others.
Team Builder	Instructs others so they learn &develop skills and approaches to ach obj's
Tolerance for Stress	Reacts to duress in balanced manner needed to sustain performance levels.

Appendix B—Corporate Entrepreneurs LLC—Product Description

Corporate Entrepreneur Profile™

The Corporate Entrepreneur Profile™ provides insights into the critical behaviors and competencies of corporate entrepreneurs. The profile enables you to leverage and develop your most entrepreneurial talent.

- Individual Profile Reports—assessment tool to identify entrepreneurial talent

- Customized Profile—tailored to the unique needs of your organization

- Critical Success Factors—key entrepreneurial behaviors and competencies

- Team Comparisons—enables you to leverage strengths and develop weaknesses

- Benchmark—compare to benchmark or create your own benchmark for success

You will increase your success rate by ensuring that the right resources are in place.

Corporate Entrepreneuring Audit™

The Corporate Entrepreneuring Audit™ helps you align systems and processes to support new business growth. The audit helps you determine which systems and processes need to be tweaked or adjusted to create an entrepreneurial environment.

- Gap Analysis—identify hidden barriers to success

- Culture Assessment—evaluate organizational flexibility and agility

- Process Evaluation—determine maturity and effectiveness of processes

- Alignment—align systems and processes to co-exist with core business

- Metrics—develop measurements that support and drive new growth

You will improve operational effectiveness by aligning people and processes for growth.

Corporate Entrepreneurial Infrastructure™

The Corporate Entrepreneurial Infrastructure™ helps you develop the entrepreneurial mindset and infrastructure for success. This action learning workshop helps you establish and develop corporate entrepreneuring as a core competency.

- Leadership Skills—develop leadership skills needed to operate differently

- Cross Functional Collaboration—create better, more acceptable ideas

- Program Management Discipline—instill discipline and leadership oversight

- Building Blocks—leverage tools and techniques

- Execution Competencies—increase buy-in and execution

You will build the entrepreneurial skills to accelerate business growth, minimize risks, and increase revenues.

Appendix C—Corporate Entrepreneuring Questions

To get an electronic copy of these questions go to www.corporate-entrepreneurs.com

Chapter 1: Next Frontier—*Corporate Entrepreneurship*

1.1 Catalyst for Growth—Corporate Entrepreneurship

Is your organization committed to becoming more entrepreneurial?

_____

1.2 Elusive Butterfly—Definition

What is your definition of corporate entrepreneurship?

_____

1.3 Growth Process—Business Process

Do you have a process in place for corporate entrepreneurship?

_____

1.4 Foundation for Success—People, Process and Place

What are you doing to develop entrepreneurial competencies?

_____

What type of operating framework will work for your organization?

_____

Does your organization have an entrepreneurial mindset and infrastructure?

_____

1.5 Pioneers—Corporate Entrepreneurs or Intrapreneurs

What processes are in place to recognize and develop corporate entrepreneurs:

_____

1.6 Extraordinary Leaders—Leadership Skills & Behaviors

Who are the entrepreneurial role models in your organization?

1.7 Building Blocks—Creativity, Innovation and Change

What ways do you encourage creativity and innovation?

How easily does your organization change?

1.8 Hitting the Target—Execution

How effective is your organization when it comes to execution?

Is benefits management an integral part of your development process?

Chapter 2: Navigating Obstacles—*Entrepreneurial Framework*

2.1 Big Picture

Is innovation a strategic priority in your organization?

Does your organization have criteria for selecting and killing new initiatives?

What processes are in place to allocate resources?

How is new business initiatives funded?

2.2 In You We Trust

Who are the entrepreneurial leaders in your organization?

What is it about their leadership style that people trust?

What programs are in place to develop more entrepreneurial leaders?

2.3 Importance of Circles

What type of organizational structure do you use for new initiatives?

What level of collaboration exists between different organizational functions?

Can you imagine organizing your next big project with interlocking circles?

2.4 Your Best Friends

How actively involved is your finance department with new initiatives?

Is the finance department viewed as a roadblock or ally?

Do you have a separate budgeting system for new initiatives?

2.5 Shifting Gears

What management systems does your organization use to support corporate entrepreneurship?

Which management systems will you need?

_____

How will they need to be changed to support your project?

_____

2.6 Obstacle Course

What types of controls are placed to manage new initiatives?

_____

What management practices get in the way?

_____

What policies and practices need to be tweaked or changed?

_____

2.7 See the Change

Does your organization have a change agenda for innovation?

_____

Is entrepreneurship a core competency?

_____

What processes are in place to create an entrepreneurial culture?

_____

Does your organization have a tolerance for failure?

_____

2.8 Champions of Change

Can you identify the corporate entrepreneurs in your organization?

_____

What are you doing to develop and nurture these individuals?

_____

What kind of incentives and rewards are in place to encourage entrepreneurial behavior?

_____

2.9 Friend or Foe

How involved is your human resource department involved in your change initiatives?

_____

2.10 Get New Glasses

What steps do you take to get the right product/service requirements?

_____

How do you guarantee that your requirements are aligned with the need?

_____

2.11 Committed to an Idea

What do you do to ensure that your organization stays committed to an idea?

_____

Chapter 3: Discipline to Succeed—*Project Management*

3.1 Equation

Is project management a strategic competency of your organization?

_____

Does your organization use a project management methodology?

_____

Does your organization use a stage gating process for product development?

_____

Do you have the skills and structured methodology to support your initiative?

_____

3.2 Playbook

What project management standards do you use to manage projects?

3.3 Stake in the Ground

Does your organization use project charters for new initiatives?

3.4 Roadmap

Are high level work plans developed and used to manage the business side of projects?

3.5 Town Crier

Do you develop communication plans for new initiatives?

3.6 Red, Yellow, Green

What techniques are you using to report on project progress?

3.7 Rules

What impact will having rules of engagement have on your projects?

3.8 Coming Up for Air

What things do you do to break the pace and create breakthrough thinking?

3.9 Illusion of Time

How does clock watching hinder or impede the progress of projects?

Is your organization focused on the end goal or tracking time?

Chapter 4: Pioneers Charting a New Course—Corporate Entrepreneurs

4.1 Similar but Different

Do you have what it takes to be a corporate entrepreneur?

4.2 Meaning of Work

Are you looking to make a difference or climb the corporate ladder?

Does your organization provide challenging opportunities?

4.3 Belonging

Are you willing to take a look at the core business in a new light?

Will you be prepared to deal with the consequences of belonging to something different?

4.4 Park Your Ego at the Door

How do you deal with prima donnas on your venture teams?

4.5 Can Do Attitude

How do you instill a can do attitude into your venture teams?

4.6 Relying on Intuition

Does your organization make decisions based on intuition?

_____

How comfortable are you in making decisions based on intuition?

_____

4.7 Living on the Edge

How many individuals in your organization are willing to live on the edge?

_____

4.8 Weekend Warriors

What are you doing to keep everyone's battery charged?

_____

4.9 Going Home

Are you willing to change yourself even if the organization doesn't?

_____

Are your prepared to deal with the consequences of being a corporate entrepreneur?

_____

Chapter 5: Builders Creating the Future—*Entrepreneurial Leader*

5.1 Hidden Talent

What is your organization doing to identify and develop entrepreneurial leaders?

_____

What is your organization doing to retain this critical corporate resource?

_____

5.2 Business Architects

How do you create the entrepreneurial mindset and infrastructure for success?

_____

5.3 Conductor

Can you create a high performance team that operates like a symphony?

_____

5.4 A People

Do you select A people to be your entrepreneurial leaders?

_____

Are you selecting A, B or C people for your entrepreneurial teams?

_____

5.5 Breaking Rules

How tolerant is your organization when individuals break rules?

_____

5.6 Alone on An Island

What ways are you helping your entrepreneurial leaders deal with isolation?

_____

5.7 Valley of Despair

Have you ever experienced the "valley of despair"?

_____

5.8 Willing to Be Fired

Are your entrepreneurial leaders willing to be fired?

_____

Chapter 6: Teams Engaged and Thriving—*Team Dynamics*

6.1 Hold onto Your Hat

Is your organization able to deal with the ups and downs of entrepreneurial projects?

_____

How does your organization help teams deal with stress?

_____

6.2 Me, You and Us

What role does the CEO have in your initiative?

_____

Is there a formal contracting process with sponsors?

_____

Are the roles and responsibilities of your team clearly defined?

_____

6.3 Soul of Project

Are values an integral part of your team building process?

_____

Which team values do you think are the most important?

_____

6.4 Stretching People

Is there a concerted effort in your organization to stretch and grow people?

_____

What are you doing to empower people?

_____

6.5 Two Days in Woods

What are you doing to create high performance teams?

_____

6.6 Lead By Following

As a leader do you lead by following or use traditional management practices?

_____

As a team member are you given the opportunity to make some of the tough decisions?

_____

6.7 Tell Us What to Do

Does your decision making process hinder or support new initiatives?

_____

Are you comfortable delegating decision making?

_____

Are you a calculated risk taker?

_____

6.8 Getting Unstuck

Are listening and empathy key competencies in your organization?

_____

How does your organization deal with conflict and tension?

_____

6.9 Struggle for Legitimacy

What things have you encountered when trying to establish legitimacy?

_____

What creative things have you done to establish legitimacy for your project?

___

Chapter 7: Discovery of Ideas with Value—*Creativity*

7.1 Exploration

What is behind your organizations desire to be more creative?

___

7.2 Gateway

What are you doing to create an environment where individuals can be creative?

___

7.3 Meditation

Is your organization open to allowing people time for creative thinking?

___

What ways to you use to stimulate creative thinking?

___

7.4 Conviction

Is there a strong belief in your initiative?

___

7.5 Passion

Are you passionate about what you are doing?

___

How passionate is the team and the rest of the organization?

___

7.6 Whole Brain

What does your organization do to create whole brain thinking?

7.7 Team Sport

Does your organization view creativity as a team sport?

7.8 Camp Fire

What things are you doing to inspire people to be creative?

Chapter 8: Experimentation Leads the Way—*Innovation*

8.1 Extension Cord

Are your innovations linked to the core business?

8.2 Experimentation is the Mother of Invention

Are you experimenting with innovation or are you jumping in with both feet?

8.3 Lowest Common Denominator

Do you compromise creativity out of your organizations ideas?

8.4 Resisting Temptation

Does your organization find it easier to imitate a competitor?

Are there more innovative ways to solve existing problems in the market?

8.5 Blank Page

How often do you start with a blank page when looking for new innovations?

8.6 Balancing Act

Are you doing a good job of balancing risk and innovation?

What types of risk is your organization ignoring?

8.7 Value Creation

How do you go about getting customer input into value creation?

7.8 Measures & Metrics

What measures and metrics is your organization using to drive business growth?

Chapter 9: Adaptability Opens the Door—*Change*

9.1 Change to Grow

Does your organization have the ability, willingness and readiness for change?

9.2 Fear

Does fear get in your way?

9.3 Unfreezing

How would you rate your organizations willingness and ability to change?

_____

Who are the individuals that have a high propensity to change?

_____

9.4 Fitting In

How adaptable are you?

_____

Do you have a lot of energy and stamina?

_____

9.5 Finding Yourself

What is it you see when you look in the mirror?

_____

What do you think the organization will see?

_____

9.6 Your Mission

Are you willing to take on the mission of change agent in your organization?

_____

Does your organization provide training for change agents?

_____

9.7 On Stage

Are you prepared to be in the spotlight?

_____

Chapter 10: Hitting the Target with Precision—*Execution*

10.1 Building Boats

What does your organization do to increase their ability to execute with precision?

_____

10.2 Clarity of Vision

How do you ensure that everyone is on the same page?

_____

10.3 New Directions

How do you handle change requests?

_____

10. 4 High on Closure

Do you have the right mix of skills on your team?

_____

Who are the creators, doers and implementers on your team?

_____

10.5 Target Practice

How much target practice is your organization doing?

_____

Who are the individuals who excel at execution?

_____

10.6 Benefits Matter

Is benefits management an integral part of your existing development process?

___

10.7 360° Degree View

How effective are you at leading in a three hundred and sixty degree world?

___

Bibliography

Begg, Deike. *Synchronicity: The Promise of Coincidence*. New York: Harper-Collins Publishers, 2001

Binney, George and Williams, Colin. *Leaning Into the Future: Changing The Way People Change Organizations*. London: Nicholas Brealey Publishing, 1995

Black, J.Stewart and Gregersen, Hal B. *Leading Strategic Change: Breaking Through the Brain Barrier*. New York: Prentice Hall, 2002

Blanchard, Ken and O'Connor, Michael. *Managing by Values.* Berrett-Koehler Publishers, Inc., 1997

Blanchard, Ken and Wahorn, Terry. *Mission Impossible: Becoming a World-Class Organization While There's Still Time*. New York: McGraw Hill, 1997

Bohm, David. Edited by Nichol, Lee. *On Creativity*. New York: Routledge, 1998

Breene, Tim, Mann, David and Nunes, Paul F. *The Right Place, The Right Time*. Accenture Outlook, 2005.

Charan, Ram. *Profitable Growth is Everyone's Business*. New York: Random House Inc., 2004

Collins, Jim. *Good to Great.* New York: HarperCollins Publishers, Inc., 2001

Collins, Jim and Porras, Jerry I. *Built to Last: Successful Habits of Visionary Companies.* New York: Harper-Collins Publishers, Inc., 2002

Cooke, Helen S. and Tate, Karen. *Project Management.* New York: McGraw Hill, 2005

Cooper, Dr. Robert G. and Edgett, Dr. Scott J. *Stage-Gate and the Critical Success Factors for New Product Development.* BPTrends, July 2005 pg.1

Davila, Tony, Espstein, Marc J. and Shelton, Robert. *Making Innovation Work: How to Manage It, Measure It and Profit from It.* New Jersey: Pearson Education Inc., 2006

Davis, Ian. *Learning to Grow Again.* The McKinsey Quarterly, 2004 Number 1 pg.125

Dudik, Evan M. *Strategic Renaissance: New Thinking and Innovative Tools to Create Great Corporate Strategies.* New York: Harper-Collins Publishing, Inc., 2000

Farson, Richard. *Management of the Absurd.* New York: Simon and Schuster, 1996

Freidman, Thomas L. *The World is Flat: A Brief History of the Twenty-first Century.* New York: Farrar, Straus and Giroux, 2005

Godin, Seth. Survival is Not Enough: *Why Smart Companies Abandon Worry and Embrace Change.* New York. Simon and Schuster, 2002

Godin, Seth. *The Big Moo: Stop Trying to Be Perfect and Start Being Remarkable.* New York: Penguin Group, 2005

Goldbrunner, Thomas, Hauser, Richard and Veldhoen, Steven. *The Four Dimensions of Intelligent Innovation: Winning the Race for Profitable Growth.* Booz | Allan | Hamilton, 2006

Gottfredson, Mark and Aspinall, Keith. *Innovation Versus Complexity: What is Too Much of A Good Thing?* Harvard Business Review, November 2005

Govindarajan, Vijay and Trimble, Chris. *Ten Rules for Strategic Innovators: From Idea to Execution.* Boston, MA: Harvard Business School Press, 2005

Gulati, Ranjay. *How CEOs Manage Growth Agendas*. Harvard Business Review, July-August, 2004 pg.1.

Harrison, Thomas L. *Instinct: Tapping Your Entrepreneurial DNA to Achieve Your Business Goals.* NewYork: Warner Business Books, 2005

Heerkens, Gary R. *The Business Savvy Project Manager*. New York: McGraw Hill, 2006

Jones, Laurie Beth. *Teach Your Team to Fish: Using Ancient Wisdom for Inspired Teamwork.* New York: Crown Business, 2002

Kotter, John P. and Heskett, James L. *Corporate Culture and Performance*. New York: Maxwell Macmillan, Inc.1992

Kouzes, James M. and Posner, Barry Z. *Encouraging the Heart: A Leaders Guide to Rewarding and Recognizing Others.* San Francisco, CA: Jossey-Bass, 1999

Labovitz, George and Rosansky, Victor. *The Power of Alignment: How Great Companies Stay Centered and Accomplish Extraordinary Things.* New York: John Wiley & Sons, Inc., 1997

Leifer, Richard, McDermott, Christopher M., O'Connor, Gina Colarelli, Peters, Lois S., Rice, Mark, and Veryzer, Robert W. *Radical Innovation.* Boston, MA: Harvard Business School Press, 2000.

Losier, Michael J. Law of Attraction: The Science of Attracting More of What You Want and Less of What you Don't. Victoria, Canada: Published Michael Losier, 2003.

Mair, Johanna. *Value Creation Through Entrepreneurial Activity: A Multiple Constituency Approach.* Research Paper No. 468. IESE Business School, University of Nirvana. Barcelona, Spain. September 2002

Mandel, Michael. *Why The Economy Is A Lot Stronger Than You Think: In a Knowledge-based World, the traditional measures don't tell the story.* Business Week, February 13, 2006, pp.63

Mason, Heidi and Rohner, Tim. *The Venture Imperative: A New Model for Corporate Innovation*. Massachusetts: Harvard Business School Press, 2002.

Maxwell, John C. Failing Forward: *Turning Mistakes into Stepping Stones for Success*. Nashville, Tennessee: Thomas Nelson, Inc., 2000

Maxwell, John C. *The 17 Essential Qualities of a Team Play: Becoming the Kind of Person Every Team Wants*. Nashville, TN: Thomas Nelson, Inc., 2002

McBeth, Elizabeth W. and Rimac, Tomislav. T*he Age of Entrepreneurial Turbulence: Creating Sustainable Advantages for Individuals, Organizations, and Societies in the New Century*. Corporate Entrepreneurship, ESADE MB Business Review, 2004.

McGehee, Tom. *Whoosh: Business In The Fast Lane*. Cambridge, MA: Perseus Publishing, 2001

McGrath, Rita Gunther and MacMillian, Ian C. *Market Busting: Strategies for Exceptional Business Growth*. Boston, MA. Harvard Business Review, March 2005.

McGregor, Jena. *Dawn of the Idea Czar*. Business Week, April 10, 2006

McGregor, Jena. *How Failure Breeds Success*. Business Week, July 10, 2006, pp. 42

Menkes, Justin. *Executive Intelligence: What All Great Leaders Have*. New York: HarperCollins Publishers, 2005

Morris, Michael H. and Kuratko, Donald F. *Corporate Entrepreneurship*. Florida: Harcourt, Inc., 2002

Nussbaum, Bruce. *Get Creative: How to Build Innovative Companies*. Business Week, August 1, 2005 pp.60

O'Connor, Michael, Blanchard, Ken, Edenburn, Carl and Zigarmi, Drea. *The Leader Within: Learning Enough About Yourself to Lead Others*. New York: Prentice Hall, 2005

Pinchott, Gifford, and Pellman, Ron. *Intrapreneuring in Action: A Handbook for Business Innovation*. San Francisco, CA: Berrett-Koehler Publishers, Inc., 1999

Pink, Daneil H. *A Whole New Mind: Moving from the Information Age to the Conceptual Age*. New York: Penguin, 2005

Richman, Larry. *Improving Your Project Management Skills*. New York. American Management Association, 2006

Seagal, Sandra and Horne, David. *Human Dynamics: A New Framework for Understanding People and Realizing the Potential in Our Organization*. Waltham, MA: Pegasus Communications, Inc., 1997

Slywotzky, Adrian. *The Art of Profitability*. New York: A AOL Time Warner Company, 2002.

Surowiecki, James. *The Wisdom of Crowds: Why the Many Are Smarter than the Few and How Collective Wisdom Shapes Business, Economics, Societies and Nations*. New York: Doubleday, 2004

Sternberg, Robert J. *Wisdom, Intelligence, and Creativity Synthesized*. New York: Cambridge University Press, 2003

Thornberry, Neal. *Lead Like an Entrepreneur: Keeping the Entrepreneurial Spirit Alive Within the Corporation*. New York: McGraw Hill, 2006

Verzuh, Eric. *The Portable MBA in Project Management*. New Jersey: John Wiley & Sons, Inc. 2003

Wagner, Bill. *The Entrepreneur Next Door*. Canada: Entrepreneur Media, Inc., 2006

Waugh, Barbara and Forrest, Margot Silk. *Soul in the Computer: The Story of Corporate Revolutionary*. Maui, Hawaii: Inner Ocean Publishing, Inc., 2001

Zander, Rosamund Stone. *The Art of Possibility: Transforming Professional and Personal Life*. New York: Penguin Group, 2000

About the Author

Susan Foley is Founder of Corporate Entrepreneurs LLC a management consulting firm focused on helping organizations build new growth businesses. Susan works with business executives under pressure to deliver better results from their strategic investments by helping them eliminate the barriers to success. She has spent the last twenty years helping Fortune 1000 companies, professional services firms and entrepreneurial startups develop new businesses that have generated millions in revenues.

An experienced corporate entrepreneur, Susan understands the challenges and opportunities of creating an entrepreneurial mindset and infrastructure inside an established organization. It can be a daunting task. Susan works with organizations to ensure that the right entrepreneurial skills, processes, and infrastructure are in place for success. She specializes in designing and building new businesses, opening new markets and developing new products with realistic plans that can be executed with precision.

Susan believes that many corporations do not fully understand the value of developing corporate entrepreneurship as a core competency. Corporate Entrepreneurs LLC was created to help change that. Susan also recognized that entrepreneurial leaders possess a unique combination of competencies that set them apart from traditional leaders. She developed the Corporate Entrepreneur Profile™ to show that they do. Susan also realized that many corporate entrepreneurs were choosing to leave large corporations because they were not being challenged or given the opportunities to leverage their skills. She wrote this book, Entrepreneurs Inside: Accelerating Business Growth with Corporate Entrepreneurs to tell their story.

Prior to founding Corporate Entrepreneurs LLC, Susan was Vice President of Research Services at Standard & Poor's where she built and managed a venture funded initiative to create the Industry Services business. She also held senior positions with 3M, Hewlett-Packard, Digital Equipment, Arthur D. Little and DMR Group (now Fujitsu Consulting). Susan graduated from Rochester Institute of Technology with a BS and MBA, received a post-graduate degree in Health Administration from Simmons Graduate School, and attended the Executive Management Training Program at INSEAD in France.

Index

H

handoff, 220
heuristics, 29, 40, 160
hidden barriers, 178, 225
hidden talent, 122
hierarchy, 75
high-performance team, 145
high-performance teams, 109, 153
home run, 98
human
  resource, 76
  resource department, 68
  systems, 26
  systems aspects, 69

I

idea
  generation, 169
  management, 49
ideas, 72
idea generation, 38
idea person, 173
illusion, 94, 149
impatient, 75
implementation, 40, 104, 210
implementers, 34, 207, 212, 213
incremental innovation, 23, 38, 42, 47,
    176, 184, 186, 188, 190
incubator, 23, 55, 63
independent
  agent, 119
  thinking, 101, 123, 138, 173
influence, 156
initiative, 20, 21, 24, 27, 30, 31, 35, 42,
    48, 53, 55, 57, 59, 61, 62, 68, 87,
    90, 100, 107, 112, 126, 129, 134,
    138, 145, 152, 155, 166, 199, 204,
    212, 215, 218
innovation, 20, 23, 29, 38, 39, 47, 50, 73,
    180, 187, 189, 191, 204
  external, 186
  internal, 186

key aspect of, 48
  measures and metrics, 188
  projects, 118
  roots of, 176
inspiration, 170, 172
instructiveness, 103
intensity, 114, 115
interim targets, 214
internal, 51, 55, 71, 73, 90, 112, 139, 153,
    160, 164, 171, 173, 175, 185, 187,
    190, 194, 196, 205, 210, 215
intrapreneurs. See corporate entrepreneurs
intuition, 38, 99, 104, 112, 113, 118, 162,
    196
investment, 31, 41, 48, 58, 60, 75, 104,
    183, 187, 251
isolation, 133

K

known, 193, 195, 196, 197, 205

L

law of attraction, 166
leaders, 21, 28. See also entrepreneurial
    leaders
leadership, 37, 50, 63, 100, 119, 127,
    138, 150, 177, 178, 182, 207,
    226
leading by following, 150, 151
learning, 22, 28, 32, 48, 66, 103, 143,
    147, 178, 186, 198, 212, 219
  environment, 129
left brain, 161, 162, 167, 168, 172
legitimacy, 155, 156
  establishing, 155, 156
life cycle, 48
listening, 154
living on the edge, 113
Losier, Michael
  Law of Attraction, The, 166
loyalty, 126, 206

Printed in the United States
106460LV00002B/4-12/A